I0109973

Our Gun, Our Consciousness, and the Collective

Letters from the Discussion in Prison

Ulrike Meinhof

PM

KER
SPL
EBE
DEB

Editorial Note

Some of the texts in this collection have never before been published in English. In German, Ulrike Meinhof's and other prisoners' texts are scattered among various publications that are barely accessible today. Their reproduction was often inaccurate. Misunderstandings also slipped into some of the texts published in English to date. Therefore, the translations in this collection are based on the original German documents in the archives, some of which have been made accessible only recently.

Our Gun, Our Consciousness, and the Collective: Letters from the Discussion in Prison
This edition © 2026 PM Press and Kersplebedeb

ISBN: 979-8-88744-132-0
Library of Congress Control Number: 2025931220

All rights reserved. No part of this publication may in any form be reproduced, transformed, duplicated or distributed without prior authorisation from the publishers.

Cover by John Yates / www.stealworks.com
Interior design by briandesign

10 9 8 7 6 5 4 3 2 1

PM Press
PO Box 23912
Oakland, CA 94623
www.pmpress.org

Printed in the USA.

Contents

Acronyms

AGO   Attorney General's Office.

BGS   *Bundesgrenzschutz* (Federal Border Patrol); border security police.

BKA   *Bundeskriminalamt* (Federal Criminal Bureau); the German equivalent of the FBI, particularly active in operations against the guerrilla and the left.

BKA-TE   The BKA's Terrorism Department: responsible for both the hunt for RAF members and for determining the transport and detention conditions of the prisoners from the RAF.

BND   *Bundesnachrichtendienst* (Federal Intelligence Service); the FRG's foreign intelligence service.

CDU   *Christlich Demokratische Union* (Christian Democratic Union); Germany's mainstream conservative party.

CSU   *Christlich-Soziale Union* (Christian-Social Union); Bavaria's mainstream conservative party, partner to the CDU.

GSG-9   *Grenzschutzgruppe 9* (Border Patrol Group 9); Germany's antiterrorist special operations unit, part of the BGS.

PCI   *Partito Comunista Italiano* (Communist Party of Italy).

SDS   *Sozialistischer Deutscher Studentenbund* (Socialist German Students' Federation); founded by the SPD in 1946. By the late 1960s it was an independent left-wing student federation and the most significant organization in the extraparliamenary opposition. It dissolved in 1970.

SPD   *Sozialdemokratische Partei Deutschlands* (Social Democratic Party of Germany); Germany's mainstream social democratic party.

VS   *Verfassungsschutz*; the German internal intelligence service, primary agency responsible for intelligence actions against the guerrilla and the left.

Introduction

"We are disarmed, but what they will never be able to take away from us, if we defend it tooth and nail, is our consciousness and the collective."

This volume is a compilation of texts drawn from the collective process that Ulrike Meinhof and her comrades from the Red Army Faction struggled to maintain during their years in prison. Included are letters from the prisoners' discussions, public statements, insights from their time underground, and documents drafted for their trials. Together, they provide a window into the period when the political prisoners' struggle in West Germany began to take shape, a struggle centered on their efforts to come together and preserve their collective capacity to act in prison—which included "the task to work on oneself, to struggle with oneself, and to overcome oneself" (Vera Figner).[1] The goal was to resist, to break through the isolation, to affirm their political identity, and to develop a common strategy. These texts remain relevant today.

Beginning with the first arrests, people suspected of underground activity, as well as their supporters, were systematically isolated. The prisoners were separated from one another and kept in different prisons, in cells surrounded by empty cells or in totally empty wings, until several high-security wings could be built. Everything was done to break their collective identity and make them betray it. They soon realized

---

1   Written in prison, where she spent twenty-two years for her activities in the organization Narodnaya Volia; see Vera Figner, *Memoirs of a Revolutionist* (New York: International Publishers, 1927), 193.

that these measures were part of a program designed to demoralize and destroy them—and they understood that they had to do everything possible to resist it. The terrain and conditions had changed, but not the necessity to struggle.

Ulrike was twenty-five when she dropped out of university to devote herself full time to her political activities. She had already been active for two or three years in the movement against the rearmament of West Germany and the stationing of nuclear weapons in Europe. She was among the organizers of a series of demonstrations against nuclear arms and the spokesperson for the Anti-Atomtod-Ausschuss (Committee Against Atomic Death), which mobilized against plans to equip the West German army with nuclear weapons. In 1958, as the number of demonstrations against the atom bomb increased throughout Europe, she noted that "the current struggle against nuclear armament has led many students to start reconsidering their political and social position."[2] In early 1959, as a member of the left-wing Socialist Students' Federation of Germany (SDS), she participated in the Congress against Nuclear Arms in West Berlin, where the SDS managed to assert itself against the Social Democratic Party (SPD) and its attempts to stifle the anti-nuclear movement.

A short time later, Ulrike became a member of the Communist Party of Germany (KPD). The KPD and its associated organizations had been banned three years earlier; during the leaden postwar years, all opposition was confronted with the aggressive anticommunism of the West's dominant Cold War doctrines—a wall of propaganda, chauvinism, conformity, authoritarianism, and social apathy. In West Germany, many Nazis retained their positions in business associations, ministries, the judiciary, the police, and the media. The KPD was the political organization that most consistently opposed Western imperialism and its military alliance NATO and was the only political party to defend anticolonial struggles. Most of its members came from the anti-Nazi resistance and had survived persecution, massacres, concentration camps, and exile. Many found themselves persecuted anew and ended up in prison, in exile, or forced underground, where they received the support of the East German Communist Party and other Communist Parties throughout Europe.

---

2   Semestral report for her study grant, August 1958.

Ulrike worked for several publications and became an editor and then editor-in-chief of the political magazine *konkret*. In her columns and articles, she attacked the continuity in the power structure in West Germany, the reactionary legislative initiatives (including the emergency laws that were already in the works at the time), the Springer press media monopoly, and the restoration of capitalist relations in Western Europe. She analyzed the history of fascism, US foreign policy, the role of NATO and European integration, the USSR's foreign policy, and the decolonization process as a catalyst for the emergence of a "New Left" in the capitalist centers.

In 1964, Ulrike left the KPD and *konkret*'s editorial board, although she continued to write for *konkret* and other publications while increasingly devoting her time to the production of radio and television documentaries. These were years of worldwide awakening. The assassination of Lumumba, a symbol of decolonization, racism in the US, the Cuban Revolution, and the war in Algeria all had repercussions in the capitalist centers of the West. In West Germany, the first militant actions occurred in late 1964, when the Congolese prime minister Moise Tshombe was pelted with eggs, tomatoes, and stink bombs during his state visit. That same year, the civil rights movement also triggered unprecedented mobilizations in the US. The Vietnam War was the final straw. With the spreading counterculture many things converged, and everywhere the Black Panther slogan was taken up: "Seize the time!"

Ulrike jumped into this movement with both feet, establishing contacts throughout Europe. Her articles on the politics and social issues of the day—Vietnam, German social democracy, consumer society, the media, police violence, the emergency laws, German economic interests in Iran, the women's movement, the strengths and weaknesses of the youth movement in Europe—aimed to expose the overall social context, to clarify connections and relationships, and to break through appearances. She produced documentaries on working conditions in the factories, the exploitation of women and migrants, the situation in the youth asylums, the catastrophic conditions in the schools for children with special needs. Her conceptual acuity and ability to make a point made her the most persuasive and highly regarded movement journalist in Germany. Her contributions were essential to the consciousness of the radical left that formally constituted itself as the

Extra-Parliamentary Opposition (APO) in December 1966, during a campaign to support the Vietnamese liberation struggle.

That Ulrike was also involved in the women's liberation struggle is among the things generally passed over in silence, out of the bourgeois interest in confusing emancipation with equality. She herself addressed this in her contribution to a book published in 1968:

> The striving of women for emancipation, which had much in common with that of the proletariat, and which arose at the same time, has been addressed by integrating women into an academic apparatus that has increasingly been instrumentalized against the emancipation of the working class and, thus, against the emancipation of women.
>
> Emancipation means liberation based on a change to social conditions and the abolition of the hierarchical social structure in favor of a democratic one: the abolition of the separation of capital and labor through the socialization of the means of production and the elimination of domination and servitude as a systemic social factor.
>
> The demand for equality does not call into question the social conditions underlying the inequality of people; on the contrary, it demands only the consistent application of injustice, equality within conditions of inequality: the equality of female workers with male workers, of white-collar women with white-collar men, [...] of female capitalists with male capitalists.[3]

Ulrike published her first analysis of the Vietnam War in May 1965. Solidarity with the resistance of the Vietnamese people led to the central question of how the imperialist war and propaganda machine could be effectively disrupted. In an article on the Vietnam War at the end of 1967, Ulrike talks about the need to "question the effectiveness of oppositional activity" and notes that even in West Germany there is an ever greater "desire for effectiveness." She knew what she was talking about, for at the time the first clandestine networks providing practical support to deserting GIs were formed. After participating in the organization of the International Vietnam Congress in West Berlin

---

3   "Falsches Bewusstsein," in Christa Rotzoll, ed., *Emanzipation und Ehe* (Munich: Editions Delp, 1968).

and the subsequent large-scale demonstration in February 1968, Ulrike concluded that the time had come to move "from protest to resistance."[4]

The subsequent months were marked by broad mobilizations against the Springer press and against the emergency laws.[5] However, the overall momentum of the uprising soon waned. Nonetheless, the following two years provided numerous concrete experiences. A broad range of projects emerged in which militants tried to organize themselves into autonomous structures. Ulrike and her comrades initiated a campaign against youth asylums and, among other things, got involved in an Action Council in the Märkisches Viertel, a newly created low-income suburb in West Berlin, where, with some three hundred teenagers, they occupied a building they needed for their gatherings.

First and foremost, this was a time of international meetings and discussions. What had become increasingly clear was that the unified nature of the capitalist system of domination made it impossible to separate the struggle in its centers from that in its "peripheries," where the anti-imperialist struggle was already in full swing. It was no longer enough to comment and protest; it was time for action, for testing theory in practice. The discussions culminated in the idea that it was essential to develop a revolutionary politics that could not be reintegrated by the system, to once again go on the offensive, to organize resistance, to intervene, to strike hard, concretely and effectively, with the intention of building a politico-military front in the capitalist centers. The analysis was based on the assessment that the international balance of power and conditions in the capitalist centers provided an opportunity that had to be seized.

In early 1970, militants from different political contexts met, and a group was formed that decided to initiate this process and to begin organizing underground structures as a prerequisite for securing their

---

4　Several articles on Vietnam; in *konkret* from May 1965 to May 1969.
5　The "New Left" of the 1960s was confronted from the outset with police violence and media vilification. The Springer press in particular was held responsible for the aggressive atmosphere that led to the death of a student, Benno Ohnesorg, during a demonstration against the Iranian regime in June 1967 and to the attempted assassination of student movement spokesperson Rudi Dutschke in April 1968. The latter attack triggered riots (the "Easter riots") in several cities against Springer establishments. One month later, large-scale mobilizations took place against the emergency laws, which were nevertheless adopted at the end of May 1968, against the backdrop of a worldwide protest movement.

freedom of movement and their ability to act. Their assumption was that it would be possible to undermine imperialism with attacks in its hinterland, which could help strengthen the perspective for advances on the part of the liberation movements in the Third World, and, in interaction with them, establish the conditions for a stronger revolutionary left in the capitalist centers. For Ulrike, "The issue was to preserve all that we had learned during the movement of 1967–1968 and to never again stop fighting."[6]

Things accelerated when Andreas Baader was arrested in April while attempting to procure weapons. The group felt that his imprisonment would delay the organizing process, which was still at an early stage, and decided to free him. There was also a sense that, as the first guerrilla action, liberating a prisoner would have the political effect of communicating the need for and possibilities of an underground organization. Despite hasty improvisation, the action succeeded, and Andreas was freed on May 14, 1970. This was followed by military training at an Al Fatah camp in Jordan and other preparations that culminated in the formation of the Red Army Faction. In *The Urban Guerrilla Concept*, published in May 1971, the RAF states, "Whether it is right to organize armed resistance now, depends on whether it is possible, and whether it is possible can only be determined in practice."[7]

One year later, the RAF launched a bombing campaign, primarily targeting the US army headquarters in Frankfurt and Heidelberg, seriously damaging computer equipment used to coordinate troop movements to and from Vietnam. In a May 1972 communiqué, the RAF declared: "West Germany and West Berlin shall no longer be a safe hinterland for the strategists of extermination in Vietnam. They must understand that their crimes against the Vietnamese people have created new and bitter enemies for them, and there is nowhere left in this world where they will be safe from the attacks of revolutionary guerrilla units."[8] In fact, armed movements had formed in several capitalist centers during this period.

From the outset, the existence of the RAF prompted a flood of distortions and disparaging and sexist lies in the media, which continually

---

6   Note on the formation of the RAF, July 1973.

7   André Moncourt and J. Smith, *The Red Army Faction: A Documentary History, Volume 1: Projectiles for the People* (Oakland/Montréal: PM Press/Kersplebedeb, 2009), 96.

8   Moncourt and Smith, 174.

wrote about a "Baader-Meinhof Gang," controlled by "group terror" and a hierarchical structure consisting of "ringleaders" and "followers." After the publication of *The Urban Guerrilla Concept*, the state security services planted the rumor in the media that Ulrike had committed suicide or had been murdered by her comrades. She was considered to be the "Voice of the RAF," a voice that had to be discredited, a voice that had to be silenced.

After the arrest of a number of RAF members in June and July 1972, the attempts to break them through isolation and, especially in the case of Ulrike, through psychiatrization, were accompanied by smear campaigns in the media aimed at discrediting the RAF and its politics through personalization and the denial of its collective structure.

The prisoners' first two hunger strikes against isolation took place in early 1973. The first one got Ulrike out of the silent wing at Cologne-Ossendorf prison, where she had been held in acoustic isolation for eight months. During this hunger strike, lawyers held their own hunger strike in front of the Supreme Court, and, in 1973, Committees Against Isolation Torture were formed in a number of cities across West Germany. Ulrike was returned to the silent wing again for two weeks at the end of 1973 and, along with Gudrun Ensslin, for three months in 1974, after which they were both transferred to Stuttgart-Stammheim on April 28, 1974.

For the prisoners from the RAF, the hunger strikes provided a direct experience of how they could act together despite separation and isolation. The establishment of a communication system, the *info*, led to a period of intense and lively discussions, with much reading and writing. Everyone felt the need and desire to once again fight for a collective process. Nonetheless, it remained clear that another hunger strike would be necessary to concretely break through the solitary confinement.

Meanwhile, in England, four prisoners from the Provisional IRA, Marian and Dolours Price, Gerry Kelly, and Hugh Feeney, began a hunger strike in November 1973, demanding to be transferred to Northern Ireland, where the political prisoners could be together. They broke off the strike only in June 1974, after more than five months of brutal force-feeding and the death of Michael Gaughan, who had joined the hunger strike.

In 1974, the prisoners from the RAF decided that they wanted to follow the example of this hunger strike. They understood that the conditions of the struggle had changed but not the character of the confrontation, and that this meant that they each needed to make a fresh decision to pursue this struggle and to be openly and honestly clear about it.

In late August 1974, Ulrike was transferred to West Berlin for the trial related to breaking Andreas Baader out of prison. On September 13, during this trial, she announced the beginning of the third collective hunger strike for the end of isolation and special measures. Force-feeding began in some prisons earlier than in others. In West Berlin, Ulrike and the other hunger-striking women were only observed and eventually transferred to the infirmary at the Moabit men's prison.

On November 11, Andreas Baader and Jan Raspe were transferred from different prisons to Stuttgart-Stammheim, where their trial was pending. Holger Meins was to be transferred there at the same time, but the transfer had been delayed on the instructions of the Attorney General.[9] He died on November 9, 1974, after fifty-eight days on hunger strike, having been systematically and brutally force-fed insufficient calories. For weeks, there were demonstrations across Europe in response to his death. In late November, Ulrike was returned to Stammheim prison, having been sentenced to eight years for her part in breaking Andreas out of prison. In December, Jean-Paul Sartre visited Andreas, and an International Defense Committee (IVK) was formed, with offices in France, Holland, Italy, Belgium, England, and West Germany. That same month, in an interview with the weekly magazine *Der Spiegel*, for the first and only time, the prisoners in Stammheim were able to publicly express themselves without their statements being overly distorted or censored.

In early 1975, judicial authorities signaled their total opposition to lifting isolation and the special measures under any circumstances but hinted that they would allow the association of some prisoners, while maintaining security measures. There was, however, no firm commitment. To force a decision, the prisoners went on thirst strike on February 1. A few days later, in a letter to the press, the RAF asked the prisoners to call off the strike for the time being, because it believed that

---

9   In Germany, the attorney general is the chief federal prosecutor in cases of organized crime, espionage, and "terrorism," as well as the coordinator of the intelligence agencies' media relations.

it had achieved what was politically possible and that "the prisoners' struggle [...] is now something that we must settle with *our* weapons."[10] After 145 days, the hunger strike came to an end.

On April 24, the RAF's Holger Meins Commando occupied the West German embassy in Stockholm and took hostages, demanding the release of twenty-six political prisoners. The government refused to negotiate. When the police stormed the embassy, there was an explosion and RAF member Ulrich Wessel was killed. Five other commando members were arrested. Despite serious injuries, Siegfried Hausner was flown to Stammheim prison, where he died on May 4.

On May 21, the trial of the so-called "ringleaders" began in Stuttgart-Stammheim. It was designed to be the key trial against the RAF and its politics, under the direction of the Attorney General's Office (AGO), and was presided over by a judge who had ever greater difficulty appearing to be anything other than a puppet of the state security services. The trial did not take place in the Stuttgart courthouse but in a bunker of sorts that was built especially for the purpose on the grounds of Stammheim prison. The area was surrounded by NATO barbed wire and police squads, snipers, and armored vehicles. Draconian security measures were in place at the entrance to the courtroom.

The trial began with hastily passed special laws, manipulated judicial files, and increasing pressure on the lawyers. Over the subsequent few months, trusted lawyers were disbarred, arrested, and had their offices searched and their files confiscated. Ulrike, Gudrun, Jan, and Andreas intervened in the trial several times with analyses, while the hearings got bogged down in procedural issues. In January 1976, the four made a key statement about their politics and the development of the armed struggle. At the beginning of May, they intervened during the defense motions to address West Germany's role in the imperialist system and in the Vietnam War in particular.

On May 9, Ulrike was found dead in her cell. We think that everything there is to say about that was said by Jan in the statement that we have included in this collection (see pp. 121–22).

After Ulrike's death, the psychological warfare against the prisoners from the RAF was ramped up again, both by demonizing those who were still alive and at the same time by trying to reclaim Ulrike for

---

10 Moncourt and Smith, 338.

almost everything she had fought against over the years. That is one of the reasons we decided to publish these texts, despite our reservations about focusing on individuals. They show her as she really was, what the collective meant to her, and how she fought for it. What we want above all with this collection is for Ulrike to once again be seen in the context of the group.

In July and August 1976, the defense called fourteen prisoners from the RAF to the Stammheim trial to testify about the collective structure of the group. Over the following months, Gudrun, Jan, and Andreas stopped attending the hearings. The trial came to a close at the end of April 1977 with life sentences, the first life sentences against RAF members. Shortly before sentencing, the RAF's Ulrike Meinhof Commando killed Attorney General Buback, who was held responsible for the deaths of Holger, Siegfried, and Ulrike.

The RAF's struggle continued for two decades. In 1998, the organization dissolved, the left's political circumstances having shifted sharply in the late 1980s. The prisoners nonetheless continued to struggle against isolation and for their political identity, a struggle that, like prison movements in other countries, had a lasting impact on other struggles inside and outside of the prisons. The last incarcerated RAF members from that period were gradually released from prison between 2001 and 2011.

—some of Ulrike's comrades who accompanied her on her journey

On the Effects of
the Silent Wing

Immediately after her arrest, Ulrike was isolated from all other prisoners in an empty and acoustically sealed wing of Cologne-Ossendorf prison. Isolation in this silent wing—known in German as a "Toter Trakt" or "dead wing," referring to the dead silence prevailing there—was based on the camera silens experiments with sensory deprivation, which had been carried out since the 1950s in the US and other places, including the Hamburg-Eppendorf University Clinic. Ulrike was initially released from the silent wing after eight months, in response to the first prisoners' hunger strike. One year later, she was sent back for two weeks.

Ulrike's text, in which she tried to sum up the effects of the physical and acoustic isolation, both for herself and for the others, was released by her lawyers at a press conference at the end of February 1974. At that time, she was in the wing for the third time, since February 5, 1974, although on this occasion with Gudrun Ensslin. They were both transferred to Stuttgart-Stammheim on April 28, 1974.

From June 16, 1972, to February 9, 1973

The feeling, one's head explodes (the feeling, the top of the skull will
    simply split, burst open)—
the feeling, one's spinal column presses into one's brain
the feeling, one's brain gradually shrivels up, like dried fruit, for
    example—

the feeling, one is constantly, imperceptibly, flooded, one is
    remote-controlled—
the feeling, one's associations are hacked away—
the feeling, one pisses the soul out of one's body, like when one cannot
    hold water—
the feeling, the cell moves. One wakes up, opens one's eyes: the cell
    moves; afternoon, if the sun shines in, it is suddenly still. One
    cannot get rid of the feeling of motion. One cannot tell whether
    one shivers from fever or from cold—
one cannot tell why one shivers—one freezes.
To speak at a normal volume requires an effort like that necessary to
    speak loudly, almost like that necessary to shout—
the feeling, one falls silent—
one can no longer identify the meaning of words, one can only guess—
the use of sibilants—s, sz, tz, z, sch is absolutely unbearable
guards, visits, the yard seem to be made of celluloid—
headaches—
flashes—
sentence construction, grammar, syntax—can no longer be controlled.
When writing: two lines—by the end of the second line, one cannot
    remember the beginning of the first—
The feeling of internal burnout—
the feeling that if one would say what's happening, if one wants to let
    it out, it's like throwing boiling water in the person's face, like, for
    example, boiling water that scalds and disfigures the person forever—
Raging aggressivity, for which no outlet exists. That's the worst.
Keen awareness that one cannot survive; total failure to convey this
    to others;
Visits leave no trace. A half an hour later one can only mechanically
    reconstruct whether the visit was today or last week.
Compared to this, bathing once a week means: a momentary thaw, a
    moment of relaxation—it lasts a few hours also—
The feeling, time and space are interwoven—
the feeling of finding oneself in a house of mirrors, like in an amusement
    park—to stagger—
Afterwards: incredible euphoria, that one hears something—
like the acoustic difference between day and night—

The feeling, time now flows, the brain expands again, the spinal column
    sinks down again—for weeks.
The feeling, as if one's skin had been stripped off.

From December 12, 1973, to January 3, 1974

Ears buzzing. Waking up, one feels as if one has been beaten.
The feeling, one moves in slow motion.

The feeling, finding yourself in a vacuum, as if you're encased in lead.
Afterwards: Shock. As if an iron plate had fallen on your head.

Comparisons, words that come to mind in there:
(mental) shredding—
A space-flight simulator, where the acceleration causes your skin to
flatten—
Kafka's Penal Colony—the guy on a bed of nails—
Non-stop rollercoaster rides.

The radio: it offers minimal relief, like when one, for example, reduces
one's speed from 240 to 190.

That everything exists in a cell that is in no obvious way different from
any other cell—radio, furniture, plus newspapers, books—is actually by
its implication rather aggravating: making any understanding between
the prisoner and people who do not know what acoustic isolation is
impossible.
    Also disorienting to the prisoner. (That it is white like a hospital
cell, for example, only increases the terror, but mainly because of the
silence. When one understands that, one paints on the walls.) Clearly,
in there one would rather be dead.

Peter Milberg, who was in one of these things in Frankfurt-Preungesheim
("an empty medical wing") subsequently accused his judge of "attempting" to kill him. It's true, what is going on in these places is simply a
type of "execution."

That is to say: A process of inner disintegration occurs—like something being dissolved in acid, which one attempts to slow down by concentrating on resistance, but nothing can stop it.

The insidiousness includes complete depersonalization. Nobody, except oneself, is in this state of emergency.

As means/method, it can quite clearly be compared, for instance, to that which they use against the Tupamaros: to create in them a state of nervous agitation and agony, shortly before administering pentothal—which suddenly creates a feeling of relief and euphoria. One expects the prisoner to lose self-control. To babble.

From the Discussion 1973–1974

The need for all political prisoners to be equally well informed and to be able to exchange information among themselves, despite the isolation, led to the creation of the info in 1973. Their letters were photocopied and forwarded via lawyers' mail. Letters addressed to any individual were shared with everyone.

As the prisoners came to understand the effects of isolation, it became a matter of resisting it with their full weight as human beings. There ensued an open and intense discussion about the situation and how to break through the isolation and resist. Under the existing conditions, collective hunger strikes were the only feasible option. Given the regular cell raids and the ban on collective defense that passed in early 1975, ongoing exchanges between the prisoners became increasingly difficult. Letters and documents for the preparation of trials had to be collected and brought into the prisons. The prisoners referred to these as "parcels."

The following documents from the 1973–1974 discussion address issues such as: determining the politics of the group in prison and at the trials, developing the capacity to act again, and reasserting a collective process.

That was also the subject of the confrontation with Horst Mahler in Ulrike's May 20, 1973, letter—the first letter from Ulrike in the info that reached everyone. Mahler was one of the most well-known left-wing lawyers in West Germany before he joined the RAF in the spring of 1970. In October 1970, he was arrested in West Berlin, along with Ingrid Schubert, Irene Goergens, Monika Berberich, and Brigitte Asdonk. The five were the first prisoners from the RAF and were immediately confronted with separation, transfers, and isolation. For two years, *they more or less fended for themselves, enduring the isolation rather than working together to resist it.*

In her letters to the women in West Berlin and also to Mahler, Ulrike tried to make sense of this period. At the same time, a discussion had begun about a new hunger strike, which aimed to finally change the conditions. The prisoners wanted to follow the example of the Irish prisoners who were on hunger strike from November 1973 to June 1974 on the initiative of the sisters Marian and Dolours Price. It was at this point that Mahler refused to participate and joined the KPD/AO, one of the first party-building organizations of the era. In September 1974, Monika Berberich announced his expulsion from the RAF.

Regarding Mahler
May 20, 1973

Wow! What to do?—What is completely clear is that the definition of "political prisoner" is not yet resolved, has not yet been thoroughly discussed, has not yet been grasped and conveyed, and that is something that we absolutely must do. Clearly, it is important that a correct understanding prevail, because what we want from the liberals (including the UN Human Rights Commission, the UN International Law Commission, and Amnesty International) is that this influential bunch with its function of protection finally stop prioritizing intellectuals and anticommunists, and that we force them to protect anti-imperialist combatants from torture—and, furthermore, that the comrades in the street understand the new fascism, its role in the prisons and concentration camps, the vital necessity of self-organization in the prisons, of the politicization of the prisons—i.e., the necessity of preventing the isolation of all those who resolutely resist, because their politicization depends on their integration with others, and because isolation means liquidation.

This is important and must be dealt with. We began to do this in the hunger strike statement, but what *you* are doing obstructs the process, and everything you say suggests that you don't care a bit about this job. That also goes for what you say about Merve.[1] Unbelievable nonsense

---

1   Horst Mahler asked Merve Publishing to publish a pamphlet he had written about the armed struggle, presenting it as a collective work. No RAF member in prison

about whether you should ask first and, if so, who you should ask, before putting yourself on the market—which is something all of us do—ask first—whoever you want to, someone you think and know perhaps has a clearer perspective than you do. Of course, *nobody*—just consider all those who are on hunger strike right now—will let themselves be pissed on by you and the question: And you, who do you think you are? That's what your boy scout–like formulations imply, or what? Really, anger and outrage, that's all I have.

But no, you better clearly say what's bugging you, once and for all. Better yet, stop barricading yourself in your hole atop your high horse and speak openly, for once, even if it's bitter.

Anyway, I'll start with what's bitter. And I'm telling you that I'm so angry and outraged that I'm not going to be business-like and carry it off in a way that meets your communication needs, as "emotionless" as you (*teacher!*) would like to keep things.

I think what has started to bother you, and what has happened during the two years you've been inside, is that you've been in there longer than most of us. Because nothing really happened—except the incessant activity of the pigs. On your side nothing. You played world central committee, party chairman, you invented global imperialism, discussed this and that, but it would seem that you were pretty much oblivious to what was actually happening around you.

What has been happening around you is the fact that there has been torture. Ali's story is known. Karameh's five months in a window-less cell is known. There are many other things that are probably not known, at least not to me. What I want to talk about here is Astrid's story, which in the meantime has also become my own.[2]

In August 1972, a lawyer told me that you were thinking about how to remove the fear of prison from the comrades on the outside—the struggle would continue in prison, and it wouldn't be all that bad. By that time, Astrid had already been in the silent wing in Cologne from

---

or outside knew anything about it. The pamphlet was not published by Merve but by Wagenbach Publishing under the title *Regarding the Armed Struggle in Western Europe* by a "RAF Collective," after having been clandestinely distributed under the title *Strassenverkehrsordnung* (Traffic Regulations). Ulrike has more to say about this in the following letter.

2   Ali, Karameh, and Astrid: Heinrich Jansen, Brigitte Asdonk, and Astrid Proll. Astrid was in the silent wing at Ossendorf prison in Cologne, first for four months, then for several months later on.

November 1971 to June 1972—with interruptions, okay. By that time, the lawyers had arranged for her to see a cardiologist, who, of course, determined that her heart was fine. Astrid had already passed out by then. It was known that this psycho-pig had already got his paws on her. On one of us who normally pukes as soon as one of these pigs appears—but even that, something like that happening, didn't cause you to notice the distress being experienced there.

I would clearly say that the political term for the silent wing, for Cologne, is the gas chamber. I can only say that my Auschwitz fantasies in there were realistic. My orientation in there too: my identification with the revolt that I set off in the end. If you survive a year or a year and a half in there without losing your mind, without simply dying, without collaborating, you come out the way they want you, a babbling idiot—or as Sigrist put it: "incapable of the slightest political resistance"[3] (because it's exactly what he described seeing in Cape Verde). Perhaps still boiling over with rage and hatred, but probably burned out and, in any case, unable to coordinate even two things, e.g., unable to both seal an envelope and put a stamp on it—to put it simply, you are completely finished. That is the fact of the matter. That is why every word about "the suffering" inside can only be shameless twaddle. In *Moby Dick*, Melville writes about Pip's distress at sea and his "suffering"—where, in principle, it's about the same thing (knowing what he's talking about, as the same thing happened to him after the sinking of the Pequod)—only one sentence: "My God! who can tell it?"[4]

Because the "suffering" is of course also crap, humiliation. Suffering is *always* the victory of the pigs, victimology glorifies the victory of the pigs, objectively mocking the tortured—and subjectively that's how I experienced it. The RAF's politics are about struggle, not suffering, and its solidarity is action, not pity.

Anyway, you couldn't really know what the silent wing is like—yet. That's why I'm writing this, so that everyone knows, in preparation for when the pigs put people there again, and so that we all clearly

---

3   Christian Sigrist, "Imperialismus: Provokation und Repression," in *Kursbuch* no. 32 (August 1973), 140. Christian Sigrist was a sociologist and president of the Amilcar Cabral Foundation.

4   Herman Melville, *Moby-Dick or The White Whale* (Boston: The St. Botolph Society, 1920), 391. Actually, in chapter 93, "The Castaway," Pip jumped into the sea not because of the sinking of the Pequod but because he panicked.

understand the magnitude of what still lies ahead of us: the new fascism's plan to liquidate the anti-imperialist left.

You couldn't know it in that way, and at first the person who is in it is also not able to explain concretely, precisely, what is happening. For a long time, you get tangled up in doubt about the degree and progress of your own destruction, precisely because, again and again, this thing cuts like an axe, continuously disrupting thoughts and associations, and you constantly lose your footing in the rubble.

That's the way it is, and you must have had some inkling, because, obviously, Astrid's situation was known. The lawyers knew about it more clearly than they later knew about mine. The pigs probably chose Astrid because they sensed that the tide was turning, since it was already clear that she couldn't deal with prison. In my case, it was probably because of the "M" in "BM,"[5] and because they want to put me in the nuthouse, a fact that by this point is clear. They would have succeeded by now if I had agreed to talk to the psycho-pig in January.

I resisted calling it torture for quite a while, because I always thought that the Tupamaros, who were subjected to psychotropics, would have been happy to swap places with me any time, until I realized that it's only a matter of time, a matter of months. Even then, after Preuss's[6] explanation about the silent wing, you correctly spoke of "torture" but then immediately returned to the order of the day. At any rate, I thought that the use of the word *torture* would cause all of us to jump up, to reflect, and to not let go. It is not our relationship to torture to provide a sound bite about it, and then three days later, well, to make a brilliant motion of rejection against a judge like Rehse.[7] Because from that point we are no longer interested in that sort of nonsense. Sure, I was confused as well.

During the testimony in Berlin, I went on the rampage, not least because of this—of course, first out of necessity, out of hatred for the excessive cynicism of Posser's missive,[8] as well as to put an end to the playing off of Astrid and me against each other—but also to cut *you* off,

5   At that time, referring to the "RAF" was taboo in the media and among politicians. Instead of "RAF," they used "BM" or "Baader-Meinhof-Bande" (Baader-Meinhof Gang), hoping to suggest that the 1972 arrests marked the end of the RAF.

6   Ulrich Preuss, lawyer for Astrid Proll and also briefly for Ulrike Meinhof.

7   Hans-Joachim Rehse was one of the countless Nazi judges who continued to practice after the war.

8   Diether Posser, minister of justice in North Rhine-Westphalia, officially responsible for the silent wing at Cologne-Ossendorf prison.

to the degree that I felt like I was in the middle of a forest, when, after I screamed, you said to the pigs that if one didn't have to fight them, one would pity them. Because my feelings were bloodthirsty. When I said "human experiment," I was thinking Nazi water hypothermia experiments: let's see when the person croaks.

The point is that the pigs did it to Astrid, and we were outside and didn't know. And you *must* have known something about it—nonetheless, in August 1972, you were still claiming that one didn't need to be afraid of jail, etc., when, by then, the attempted murders of Carl, Carmen, and Andreas had already taken place, Tommy had been liquidated, Jan and Holger had been beaten, and Gerd had been "interrogated" in the presence of his parents.[9] There you are still talking such shit! What do you see at all? What do you perceive at all? Why didn't all of you, why didn't *you*, organize a hunger strike against your isolation much earlier, against the mess forced upon each of you. Why didn't you organize to publicly expose Astrid's isolation?

You resist the term "political prisoner," but you claim it like a possession, a title to own. The activity behind the term, which is now on the table, which *demands* acting in solidarity—you simply see that from your perspective. You treat it as a source of "controversy," rather than self-critically examining *yourself*.

Your key sentence is: "Every struggle must unequivocally be a struggle for the interests and needs of the masses"—there is no more meaningless and pompous word than *unequivocally*—but if, out of fetishization of the masses or, let's say, pure kitsch, you can't even see the comrades, then you can puff yourself up by claiming to be a cadre, but you aren't. "Everyone within the ranks of the revolution must lovingly care for each other," Mao says in *Serve the People*[10]—and that surely includes the comrades—first and foremost—doesn't it?

Furthermore, you respond to nothing. You answer questions about Merve juristically and criminologically, saying that you were not made aware of the afterword and the defamatory scribbling that had been added. When asked about your activity, you are simply evasive, and you ignore the quite clearly formulated question: "Why, if everything is so

---

9   Carl (Manfred Grashof), Carmen, Andreas, Tommy, Jan, Holger, Gerd: members of the RAF. See the Chronology at the end of this volume.
10 Mao Zedong, "Serve the People" (September 8, 1944), in *Selected Works of Mao-Tse-tung*, vol. 3 (Beijing: Foreign Languages Press, 1965), 228.

simple, have there not already been four hundred or four thousand hunger strikers in the prisons?"—among whom you, obviously, would not have been one. That, among other things, is, however, also a question for *you*!

After we were interrogated in Berlin, you wrote that you had come to understand a hell of a lot about yourself, your opportunism, the market, your maneuvering, and your problems. What you do, the way you behave, is not what you want, but you must see what's going on with yourself and, above all, what's not going on, and that's why I say: "Finally, speak bitterly"—rather than hiding behind issues that are not at all your problem right now.

The unfocused, pointless nonsense that you have spouted on the subject of controversy cannot be the result of a few days of not eating but is twisted and warped and is only one of the many layers of armor within which you encase yourself.

What I'm trying to say is stop with the bullshit psychoanalysis, because there is only one liberation from the many kinds of death in this system and only one cure for the colonial, fascist, exploitative, and market neurosis—and that is violence against the pigs: our gun, our consciousness, and the collective. We are disarmed, but what they will never be able to take away from us, if we defend it tooth and nail, is our consciousness and the collective. And consciousness is not book knowledge but hatred, class hatred for the pigs and for everything that prevents us from putting this hatred into practice. That includes the torture and most certainly the fact that they have been isolating you for so long, the *cell*, the incessant terror to which you are exposed and which terrorizes you all the more the less you grasp it and the more you imagine that it doesn't really bother you all that much.

Them or us—them for themselves or us for ourselves—either you are part of the problem or you are part of the solution.

Regarding Mahler and His Writings Once Again
July 22, 1974

I have no particular interest in tearing apart those *Traffic Regulations*.[11]

---

11 The pamphlet written by Horst Mahler. It was distributed surreptitiously under the title *Traffic Regulations* before being published by Wagenbach Publishing.

It's also incorrect when you say that everyone has to do so themselves. That's no longer relevant. By the time it came out we thought it was crap, if only because it came across as so ambitiously academic and ML in style.[12] And because it declared: without theory, the revolution cannot be victorious, which was/is clearly a betrayal, because the RAF means practice and armed anti-imperialist struggle, not another theory. Therein also lies the alienated relationship to theory: incantations, Mao recited like a prayer, and concrete analysis demanded, but precisely not being produced. Also: the ML market, the pulpit, the HR manager, the supervisor, the preacher, but not the producer himself.

He does what he has always done: quoting the classics as authorities instead of allies, as a wagging finger for enlightenment instead of for the struggle. But what our thing must always be is: a weapon—to unmask the fascists, disarm the opportunists, polarize the scene, identify the enemy, separate friend from foe.

"Between the sheets"—that's where his bourgeois concept of politics comes into its own: gentlemen's club, separation of politics from private life. The old one who wants it all, except for one thing: to become a new person.

We didn't condemn or denounce this thing—James fishing in the pond of the student left[13]—when it came out without our knowledge. It's of little importance that the opportunist left can jump on *Traffic Regulations* and its empty phrases after having been forced by the existence of the RAF to think differently—that is, to think not just in terms of political economy (or whatever it understands that to be), for once, but, rather, in terms of dialectical materialism. Our practice relativized the nonsense from the beginning, and had they (e.g., *Hochschulkampf*) not had these phrases,[14] they would have pulled something out of thin air. We never identified with this pamphlet, so distancing ourselves only matters to those on the outside.

---

12 ML: parties that referred to themselves as Marxist-Leninist.

13 Both "the old one" and "James" refer to Horst Mahler.

14 In the early 1970s, *Hochschulkampf* was the newspaper of several student groups in West Berlin that were organized into "red cells."

Because the laws of the market rule in these *Traffic Regulations*, there was also no learning process for him, as was clear in his October 9, 1972, statement—that is, after May 1972.[15]

(Apart from the fact that it is fundamentally wrong to respond to the contents of opportunist bullshit, because its roots lie not in the rhetoric but in the internalized self-alienation that rationalizes all his blather and, through his complicity and conscious or unconscious identification with the enemy [however mediated], is the voice of the system—or, as Engels defines ideology: "Ideology is a process which is, it is true, carried out consciously by what we call a thinker, but with a consciousness that is spurious. The actual motives by which he is impelled remain hidden from him, for otherwise it would not be an ideological process."[16] Unmasking all this, of course, inevitably involves attacking the class roots of the rationalization of the individual concerned [which is the most frowned upon thing in bourgeois communication—getting personal instead of remaining objective, in keeping with the motto: "We are pigs in any case and will remain so."])

The truly anti-RAF position in these *Traffic Regulations*—repeated in his October 9 statement—is that he proposes not an urban guerrilla but a neighborhood guerrilla—so not, as Lenin, for example, says (reflected in the RAF's policy): to "work out a strategy that is on a level with the best international strategy of the most advanced bourgeoisie, which is 'enlightened' by age-long experience."[17]

Instead, there is a strategy that he imagines the masses would go for, "holding landlords accountable" and the little bosses "responsible" (because—and this is the core of mass opportunism—the masses would be "too stupid" to work on a strategy at the level of those worked out by the Pentagon and Fort Bragg), which, after May 1972, was treason, was counterrevolutionary. You may be hard of hearing and obtuse, but if

---

15 May 1972 refers to the RAF offensive which consisted of a number of bombings, most notably of US military installations. Mahler made his October 9, 1972, statement at the beginning of the trial against him for "membership in a criminal organization," calling for the "punishment" of enemies of the people and criticizing the Black September Organization for not taking German Foreign Affairs minister Hans Genscher as a hostage during their action at the 1972 Olympic Games in Munich.

16 Frederick Engels, "Engels to Franz Mehring" (July 14, 1893), in *Marx and Engels Collected Works*, vol. 50 (London: Lawrence & Wishart, 1975), 164.

17 V.I. Lenin, "A Letter to the German Communists" (August 14, 1921), in *Collected Works*, vol. 32 (Moscow: Progress Publishers, 1965), 513-14.

even the explosion of TNT can't wake you up, then you no longer *want* to hear anything. In which case, let the dead bury the dead, and we won't pay you any further mind.

What's more: it is also clear why he always put so much emphasis on the fact that even under imperialism there are contradictions and competition between the monopolies—which nobody denies. But the essential thing in imperialism is that within the bourgeoisie there is no serious element of power, no influential faction, outside of the monopolies. The totalitarianism of monopoly capital has simplified the matter into two possible positions, classes, perspectives: socialism or barbarism, revolutionary or fascist. Whether bourgeois democracy or a military junta, it is the policy of monopoly capital that determines governments and their practice: expansion and domination, fascism. And the opportunist left, whether it likes it or not, in its identification with the enemy is objectively tending to become a faction of fascism.

Of course, James's whole contradictions-in-imperialism and competition-of-monopolies trip was meant to provide an economic justification for his own opportunism. As if between the problem and the solution there was still, in some way or another, room for parliamentarism, diplomacy, reformism, AO, ML, etc., or any other existential approach besides finally being with and working as part of the guerrilla. Given the contradictions within the judiciary and among the lawyers, he could in fact do nothing but use them against us. Mystifying banalities and making much ado about nothing are also forms of liberalism.

His final great discovery: "the world is full of crooks"—providing a single, huge, inexhaustible clientele for all the lawyers and gendarmes—similar to all of the sainted Doctor Huber's sick people[18]—in the name of the market and the BKA's "social-sanitary epistemic privilege."[19]

In the real world, Confucians eat people—"Wanting to eat men, at the same time afraid of being eaten themselves, they all look at each other with the deepest suspicion" (Lu Xun).[20]

---

18 Wolfgang Huber was one of the founders of the Socialist Patients' Collective (SPK), whose motto was: "turn illness into a weapon." Several individuals who had been active in the SPK would later join the RAF.

19 The "social-sanitary epistemic privilege" was something asserted by BKA chief Horst Herold. The BKA is Germany's federal investigation bureau.

20 Lu Xun, "A Madman's Diary" in *Lu Xun Selected Works* (Beijing: Foreign Languages Press, 2007).

That's the way it is with competition and contradictions within imperialism.

In the final analysis, the RAF's theory should always be its practice, as Andreas said a year and a half ago.

James—this simply must be acknowledged—has broken with our practice, because armed struggle and revolutionary upheaval do not exist without self-transformation and struggle-criticism-transformation.

He was finished by the criticism from Ali and the ones in the Lehrter,[21] who, according to his projections, which resemble those of the BKA ("Mahler's girls"), occupy the lowest rung in the RAF. Of course, his hatred for us reflects his hatred for and fear of the people. He could identify with the petty-bourgeois twats in the tower,[22] could cast his pig's eye view there, but when those ladies began to behave like revolutionaries again, he freaked out. While Huber is a man-eater without a gun, Mahler is a pacifist with a gun. The one clings to bourgeois methods and ignores the cops—boycott and embargo—the other carries the gun as a status symbol. To hell with these chameleons, lodge brothers, and buddhas.

To the Women in West Berlin
August 22, 1974

You should stop localizing the problems, the petty bourgeois psycho stuff, in the tower. It's been a long time since it had anything to do with the tower.

A lot of that is just reified practice—under the rubric of "if only." It's as if you might have been spared some of the struggle if you had only fought in the tower. Nonsense. It's also a—surely unconscious—division

---

21 "Ali" refers to Heinrich Jansen, arrested in December 1970; "Lehrter" refers to the women prisoners from the RAF who were at the Lehrterstrasse prison in West Berlin: Ingrid Schubert and Irene Goergens, who were joined there by Brigitte Asdonk and Monika Berberich in 1972.

22 The "tower" was a high-security section in the Moabit men's prison in West Berlin where the women prisoners were held on a number of occasions, including during their trials. Ingrid Schubert, Irene Goergens, and others were moved in and out at least six times over a period of six years. See Ingrid Schubert, *Letters from Prison 1970–1977* (Oakland/Montréal: PM Press/Kersplebedeb, 2025), 60, 94, 97–98, 189–90, 196, 197–99, 213, 214–16.

that you create for yourselves: anyone who hasn't been in the tower doesn't know what's really going on. Bullshit. Untrue. That would be the same as me blathering on about the silent wing. What has actually happened in these brainwashing factories is not clarified by continuing to rummage around in them but by adopting the revolutionary proletarian perspective, revolutionary morality—by freeing oneself with revolutionary morality from the agony and bourgeois guilt and by learning to resist.

In this context: "Our sensation, our consciousness is only an image of the external world, and it is obvious that an image cannot exist without the thing imaged. [...] This is materialism: matter acting upon our sense-organs produces sensation. Sensation depends on the brain, nerves, retina, etc., *i.e., on matter organized in a definite way.* The existence of matter does not depend on sensation. Matter is primary. Sensation, thought, consciousness are the supreme product of matter organized in a particular way. Such are the views of materialism in general, and of Marx and Engels in particular." (Lenin, *Materialism and Empirio-criticism*)[23]

Meaning, Nelly,[24] that that's where you have to start—with the way things *are*. To acknowledge that and then to change it, to change yourself. In any case, imperialism is to blame when anyone is broken. As long as you make excuses for yourself, you make excuses for imperialism, so it's time you became a materialist.

To Nelly and the Other Prisoners in West Berlin
August 25, 1974

Nelly, your seven lines in the *info* are a way of looking forward while going backward. Your mistake is not "minor," and you cannot "always take" the class point of view—the view from below, taking a strategic position in the people's war, being militant, all mean the same thing—without having assimilated it.

We do not flee from compromise, the bourgeoisie, and betrayal; we resist them. The way you see things, you still have the cops on your

---

23   V.I. Lenin, *Materialism and Empirio-criticism* (May 1909), in *Collected Works*, vol. 14 (Moscow: Progress Publishers, 1972), 55, 69.
24   "Nelly" was Monika Berberich's pseudonym.

back; that is, you fear betrayal, the bourgeoisie, and compromise, so you still cling to bourgeois morality and, more generally, to fear.

You must resist the fear. Because, lest you have any doubt, fear lies at the core of the pressure to perform, the compulsion that spoils everything.

Reflexes—without quotation marks—means that the feelings, the emotions, the spontaneous reactions that in someone who has not completely turned him or herself inside out, stood on his or her own two feet, broken with the bourgeoisie, conquered a strategic position in the people's war, are simply wrong, not commensurate with the reality of the revolution, not geared to victory, but are still determined by the flawed logic of the system: everyone against everyone, competition; instead of learning from mistakes, justifying them; instead of learning from criticism, first searching out its inaccuracies; instead of first thinking, immediately becoming angry. All this in one word: *self-alienation*.

It is, of course, disheartening that you have seemingly engaged in the learning process that has been going on for months through the *info* but have not seen it as having anything to do with you. I don't know how you managed that. Maybe it is because in the Lehrter you are more or less together and are, therefore, not in such an unforgiving situation (but only *apparently* so) as those who are completely isolated.

In any case, keep at it, and don't let up until you have it. Let this be your reality: continuous struggle, twenty-four hours a day, defending the revolutionary inside you by finally waging war on the pig inside you. "Upheavals take place in dead ends."[25]

Of course, you have to figure out for yourself where to begin. The main thing is that you don't let up in the slightest—ever.

A tactical goal, for example, could be that you get yourself to the point where you stop feeling threatened if the pigs lock you in the tower again. To begin with, completely let go of what happened in the tower. As Thuan says in *Poulo Condor*, "All that matters is the moment and how you get through it."[26]

25 Bertholt Brecht, *Buch der Wendungen*, in *Gesammelte Werke in 20 Bänden*, vol. 12 (Frankfurt am Main: Suhrkamp 1967), 515. Translation by the editors.

26 Nguyen Duc Thuan, *Poulo Condor or the Sense of Life*, an East German radio feature on the "tiger cages" at the Poulo Condor prison in Vietnam. The transcript was distributed in the *info*; see Pieter Bakker Schut (ed.), *das info* (Kiel: Neuer Malik Verlag, 1987), 322–34, socialhistoryportal.org/raf/5429. The radio feature was based on Nguyen Duc

Hic Rhodus. Hic salta.[27]

As to your criticism of the hunger strike statement: I still have to think about it, but why didn't you rewrite it yourself?

But I don't know whether it can still be used like that at all. Damn—because now I am also working on my statement and still struggling with the remnants of the old and the wrong. Based on the actual situation, the right thing for me to do is to concentrate on the statement right now, and it is laziness on your part if you do not even try to write something like that yourselves.

Early September 1974

Damn—I'll send something along here. I don't think it's that bad. However, I'm not at all satisfied or all that sure of it, but it clarifies how I conceive of it. I can still add to it, etc., in one way or another.

It's pretty clear that the old writing doesn't work anymore, and the new one isn't there yet. But it's also because, initially, I didn't have a good understanding of the guerrilla/state issue; although, if you take the strategy of revolution in the capitalist centers—the guerrilla against the state, the smashing, annihilation, and utter destruction of the state apparatus—you can find it all in Lenin.[28] Well, this terrible fusion of parliamentarism and Marxism, the alienated definition of practice held by all groups not fighting with arms against the state.

I agree, Jimmy:[29] we *need* the word *resistance*. What is it that we do twenty-four hours a day in the box if not *resist*? *Liberation* is the word—not *freedom*. In any case, we can only imagine what freedom is. It is what is beginning to come into being in our relationships—and we can't talk about that.

Heavens. With this kind of writing, it's not a matter of getting all kinds of details and individual thoughts across. It's a matter of

---

Thuan's book *Bat Khuat* (Indomitable), published in French as *Indomptable* (Hanoi: Foreign Languages Publishing House, 1972).

27   "Rhodes is here, leap here!" is a quotation from one of Aesop's fables taken up by Hegel and later by Marx in *The Eighteenth Brumaire of Louis Bonaparte*.

28   V.I. Lenin, "The State and Revolution" (1918), in *Collected Works*, vol. 25 (Moscow: Progress Publishers, 1964).

29   "Jimmy" was Holger Meins's pseudonym.

expressing one's identity. Facts present a similar issue. They quickly become commodities—evidence, proof, examples, shit.

Well—the vertical class analysis.[30] In the learning process, at least for me, it was incredibly important. Nonetheless, I don't see us talking about something like that.

It's about the liberation of labor—and about smashing, destroying the state apparatus. Thus: Paris manuscripts[31]/Lenin's "State and Revolution"/guerrilla/RAF and explosions in the prison system, the strongest point in the imperialist state.

What the architecture is in Ossendorf, the cops are here in Moabit. A brutal bunch. Nevertheless, the orientation is easier—the orientation, not the fight. Anyway, enough.

I don't know, really. I only know one thing at this point: where you pulled me out of, from May to the end of August—I can't say any more about that.

From the abyss.

Regarding the First Day of the Trial
September 10, 1974

Mahler today. Well—horrible. A mask, completely identical to the judicial masks, was also addressed by I don't know who as a "former lawyer." He then made a terribly hollow speech on the subject of court-imposed lawyers,[32] which I listened to—in the style of: "I'll explain this here, because a layman wouldn't understand it otherwise."

Once again, I slipped him a note: "Not a word about the RAF. Otherwise, it gets ugly, you lawyer."

When he was done, the AO choir in the back stood up[33]—entirely in keeping with the justice ritual, they chanted, "Acquit

---

30 "Vertical class analysis" refers to a letter by Jan Raspe in the *info*, where he develops a notion of class that explains the divisions within the different social classes as "vertical, so to speak"; see Pieter Bakker Schut, ed., *das info* (Kiel: Neuer Malik Verlag, 1987), 116–23, 141–43, https://socialhistoryportal.org/raf/5579.

31 "The Paris manuscripts" refers to Karl Marx, *Economic and Philosophic Manuscripts of 1844* (Chicago: Dover Publications, 2007).

32 In trials of RAF members, court-imposed lawyers were supposed to formally defend the accused if their chosen lawyers were excluded or refused to participate.

33 The KPD/AO was one of the first self-styled Marxist-Leninist groups of the era.

Mahler-Meinhof-Bäcker!" and "Down with bourgeois class justice!"[34] So: *unimaginable* that there might be any good people in tow with that bunch. Funeral choirs.

At the beginning of the first break, I said a bit foolishly that I requested my exclusion, so I wouldn't have to listen to the monkey business, but I was ignored. Well, shit. I couldn't force them to exclude me, because then they exclude you right to the end. So that can't happen until Friday.

To revisit: a few days ago, when I outlined how facts quickly become currency—that was nonsense. I made a rule out of my momentary problem. Well, for a petty bourgeois, existentialism can, of course, be a pathway to dialectical materialism—but then one must also rapidly arrive at the facts, otherwise the existentialist approach becomes a religion, and approached in this way the inverse is also true.

The AO shit today has also finally made it clear to me that the defensive beginning of my statement lags four years behind reality. I must change it. As you say: not the guerrilla—but Feuerbach.

I would say that and if I'm also struggling with form at the moment, it is the result of my own disequilibrium. In this way, this trial day was also an experience, i.e., of the space in which what I say will be received—and their desire to denounce it without even batting an eye.

I must say that I no longer understand our outrage in Cologne about these people, these puffed up egos. They're *all* like that. Schily[35]— with his raised, quivering voice—wow, how empty and ridiculous it all is.

I wrote to Mahler and told him that he has until Friday to explain how he intends to avoid being used against us in the framework of what he is doing, but I don't think he will respond. He feels comfortable and safe. Bowing and scraping in front of the cops—effectively.

Lehrter again. That's all correct—but the political concepts are missing. Damn. You just can't get around political schooling, Mao, etc., and also, radical is not the same as revolutionary.

---

34   Horst Mahler, Ulrike Meinhof, and Hans-Jürgen Bäcker were accused in this second trial in connection with the Andreas Baader prison breakout. Ingrid Schubert and Irene Goergens had already been convicted at the first trial in May 1971.

35   Otto Schily was one of the chosen defense lawyers.

Statement Regarding the Liberation of Andreas from Prison

Ulrike made this statement on September 13, 1974, when on trial in connection with the Andreas Baader prison breakout. That same day, she announced the political prisoners' third collective hunger strike against their isolation. The strike would continue until February 5, 1975.

This trial is a tactical maneuver, a part of the psychological war being waged against us by the BKA, the AGO, and the justice system:

- with the goal of obfuscating both the political ramifications of our trials and the AGO's extermination strategy in West Germany;
- with the goal of using separate convictions to create the appearance of division, by putting only a few of us on display at any one time;
- with the goal of concealing the political context of all trials against prisoners from the RAF from the public;
- with the goal of forever eliminating from the people's consciousness the fact that on the terrain of West German imperialism and in West Berlin there is a revolutionary urban guerrilla movement.[1]

We from the RAF will not participate in this trial.

---

1   The preceding points appeared in the German as one long paragraph; they have been reformatted here for added readability.

The Anti-Imperialist Struggle

If it is to be more than just an empty slogan, the struggle against imperialism must aim to destroy, to disrupt, to smash the system of imperialist domination—on the political, economic, and military planes. It must aim to smash the cultural institutions that imperialism uses to bind together the ruling elites and the communications structure that ensures their ideological control.

In the international context, the military destruction of imperialism means the destruction of US imperialism's military alliances throughout the world, and here that means the destruction of NATO and the German army. In the national context it means the destruction of the state's armed formations, which embody the ruling class's monopoly of violence and its state power: the police, the BGS,[2] the intelligence services. On the economic plane, it means the destruction of the power structure that represents the multinational corporations. On the political plane, it means the destruction of the bureaucracies, organizations, and power structures, whether state or non-state (parties, unions, the media), that dominate the people.

Proletarian Internationalism

The struggle against imperialism here is not and cannot be a national liberation struggle. Socialism in one country is not its historical perspective. Faced with the transnational organization of capital and the military alliances with which US imperialism encircles the world, the cooperation of the police and the secret services, the way the dominant elite is organized internationally within US imperialism's sphere of power—faced with all of this, our side, the side of the proletariat, refers to the struggle of the revolutionary classes, the people's liberation movements in the Third World,[3] and the urban guerrilla in the imperialist centers. That is proletarian internationalism.

Ever since the Paris Commune, it has been clear that a people who seek to liberate themselves within the national framework in an

---

2   Bundesgrenzschutz: border security police.
3   The term "Third World," which was coined by French sociologists to designate the Non-Aligned Movement that emerged from the Bandung Conference in 1955, was at the time transformed into a battle cry by the anticolonial and anti-imperialist movements. In our opinion, it cannot be transformed into "Global South," as the latter term merely designates a geographic zone of neocolonial dependency.

imperialist state attract the vengeance, the armed might, and deadly hostility of the bourgeoisie of all the other imperialist states. That is why NATO is currently putting together an intervention force, to be stationed in Italy, with which to respond to internal difficulties.

Marx said, "A people which oppresses another forges its own chains."[4] The military significance of the urban guerrilla in the capitalist centers—the RAF here, the Red Brigades in Italy, and the United Peoples Liberation Army[5] in the USA—lies in the fact that it can attack imperialism here in its rear base, from where it sends its troops, its arms, its instructors, its technology, its communication systems, and its cultural fascism to oppress and exploit the people of the Third World. That is the strategic starting point of the guerrilla in the capitalist centers: to unleash the guerrilla, the armed struggle against imperialism, and the people's war in imperialism's rear bases, to begin a long-term process. Because world revolution is surely not an affair of a few days, a few weeks, a few months, not an affair of a few popular uprisings, a short process, a matter of taking control of the state, as the revisionist parties and groups imagine and claim, insofar as they imagine anything at all.

The Notion of the Nation-State

In the capitalist centers, the notion of the nation-state has become a hollow fiction, given the reality of the ruling classes, their policies, and their structure of domination, which no longer has anything to do with linguistic divisions, as there are millions of immigrant workers in the rich countries of Western Europe. The current reality—given the globalization of capital, given the new media, given the mutual dependencies that support economic development, given the growth of the European Community, and given the crisis—while remaining subjective, greatly encourages the formation of European proletarian internationalism, to the point that the unions have worked for years to box it in, to control it, to institutionalize it, and to repress it.

---

4 Karl Marx, "General Council Circular to the Roman Swiss Federal Council" (January 1, 1870), in German in *Marx Engels Werke*, vol. 16 (Berlin: Dietz Verlag, 1962), 389. Similarly, Frederick Engels, "A people that oppresses others cannot emancipate itself"; Frederick Engels, "A Polish Proclamation" (June 11, 1874), in *Marx and Engels Collected Works*, vol. 24 (London: Lawrence & Wishart, 1975), 11.

5 Ulrike probably meant the Symbionese Liberation Army.

The fiction of the nation-state, to which the revisionist groups are attached with their organizational form, is in keeping with their fetish for legality, their pacifism, and their massive opportunism. We are not reproaching the members of these groups for coming from the petty bourgeoisie, but for reproducing, in their politics and in their organizational structure, the ideology of the petty bourgeoisie, which has always been hostile to proletarian internationalism—their class position and conditions of social reproduction cannot be seen otherwise. They are always organized within the state as a complement to the national bourgeoisie, to the dominant class.

As for ourselves—we from the RAF, revolutionary prisoners detained in isolation, in special units, subjected to highly structured and completely illegal brainwashing programs in prison, as well as those underground—the argument that the masses are not yet sufficiently advanced just reminds us of what the colonialist pigs have been saying about Africa and Asia for the past seventy years. According to them, Blacks, illiterates, slaves, colonized peoples, torture victims, the oppressed, and the starving, who suffer under the yoke of colonialism and imperialism, are not yet advanced enough to control their own administration like human beings. According to them, they are not yet advanced enough to control their own industrialization, their own education, their own future. This is the argument of people concerned with their own positions of power, those who want to rule the people, who are not concerned with emancipation and the struggle for liberation.

The Urban Guerrilla

Our action on May 14, 1970, was and remains an exemplary action for the urban guerrilla. It contained all of the elements required for a strategy of armed struggle against imperialism. It served to free a prisoner from the grip of the state. It was a guerrilla action, an action of a group that, in deciding to carry it out, organized itself as a politico-military cell. They acted to free a revolutionary, a cadre who was and remains indispensable to organizing the guerrilla in the capitalist center. And not only indispensable like every revolutionary is indispensable in the ranks of the revolution, for already at this stage, he embodied everything that made the guerrilla possible, that made possible the politico-military offensive against the imperialist state. He embodied the determination, the will to act, the ability to orient himself solely and exclusively in terms of the objectives, while leaving space for the collective learning process, and practicing leadership collectively right from the start, mediating between each person's individual experience and the collective as a whole.

The action was exemplary, because the anti-imperialist struggle is about liberation: from the prison that the system has always been for all exploited and oppressed strata of the people, who have no historical perspective except that of death, terror, fascism, and barbarism. To liberate them from their imprisonment within the most complete and utter alienation, from their self-alienation, from the state of political and existential disaster in which the people are obliged to live while in the grip of imperialism, of consumer society, of the media, and of the ruling-class structures of social control, where they remain dependent on the market and the state.

The guerrilla—and not only here: it is the same in Brazil, in Uruguay, in Cuba, and for Che in Bolivia—always starts from point zero, and the first phase of its development is the most difficult. Neither the bourgeois class prostituted to imperialism, nor the proletariat colonized by it, provide anything of use to us in this struggle. We are a group of comrades who have decided to act—to break with the stage of lethargy, of purely rhetorical radicalism, of increasingly vain discussions about strategy—and to fight. We are lacking in everything, not only all the means: it is only now that we are discovering what sort of human beings we are. We are individuals in the capitalist centers, who come out of a process of the system's decay, the alienated, false, poisonous relationships that it creates in our lives—the factories, the offices, the schools, the universities, the revisionist groups, the apprenticeships, and odd jobs. We are discovering the effects of the division between professional life and private life, the division between intellectual labor and manual labor, incapacitation through hierarchical working conditions, the psychological deformations produced by consumer society, the society in the capitalist centers that are sliding into decline and stagnation.

But that is who we are, that is where we come from. We are the offspring of metropolitan annihilation and destruction, of the war of all against all, of the conflict of each individual with every other individual, of a system governed by fear, of the compulsion to produce, of the profit of one to the detriment of others, of the division of people into men and women, young and old, sick and healthy, foreigners and Germans, and of the struggle for prestige. That's where we come from: the isolation in row houses, the concrete silos of the suburbs, the prison cells, the asylums and special units, media brainwashing, consumerism, corporal punishment, the ideology of nonviolence, depression, illness, class degradation, the debasement and humiliation of the human being, of all exploited people under imperialism. Until we understand the distress of each one of us as the necessity to liberate ourselves from imperialism, as the necessity of anti-imperialist struggle. And understand that we have nothing to lose by destroying the system, but everything to gain from armed struggle: collective liberation, life, human dignity, identity. That the cause of the people, the masses, the assembly-line workers, the lumpen proletariat, the prisoners, the apprentices—the lowest masses here and the liberation movements in the Third World—is our cause. Our cause—armed struggle against imperialism—is the masses' cause and vice versa, even if it can only become a reality through a long-term process whereby the politico-military offensive develops and people's war breaks out.

That is the difference between being truly revolutionary and claiming to be revolutionary but in reality holding opportunist politics: we start from the objective situation, from the objective conditions, from the actual situation of the proletariat and the masses in the capitalist center, from the fact that all layers of society are in all ways under the system's control. The opportunists base themselves on the alienated consciousness of the proletariat; we start from the fact of alienation, from which follows the necessity of liberation.

In 1916 Lenin responded to the colonialist renegade pig Kautsky:

> No one can seriously think it possible to organize the majority of the proletariat under capitalism. Secondly—and this is the main point—it is not so much a question of the size of an organization, as of the real, objective significance of its policy: does its policy represent the masses, does it serve them, i.e., does it aim at their liberation from capitalism, or does it represent the interests of the minority, the minority's reconciliation with capitalism?
>
> Neither we nor anyone else can calculate precisely what portion of the proletariat is following and will follow the social-chauvinists and opportunists. This will be revealed only by the struggle, it will be definitely decided only by the socialist

revolution. And it is therefore our duty, if we wish to remain socialists to go down lower and deeper, to the real masses; this is the whole meaning and the whole purport of the struggle against opportunism.[6]

The Individual Guerrilla Is the Group

The role of leadership within the guerrilla, the role of Andreas in the RAF, is to provide orientation. It is not only a matter of distinguishing what is essential from what is secondary in each situation but also of knowing how to connect each situation to the greater political context by elaborating its particularities, while never losing sight of the goal—revolution—as a result of details or specific technical or logistical problems, never losing sight of the overall tactical or strategic politics of the alliance, the question of class. This means never falling into opportunism.

This, said Le Duan, is "the art of dialectically combining firmness of principle with flexibility of policy and applying to the work of revolutionary leadership the law of development from gradual changes to 'leaps'."[7] It is also the art of not "recoil[ing] again and again from the indefinite prodigiousness of [our] own aims,"[8] but of pursuing them stubbornly and without allowing yourself to be discouraged. It is the courage to draw lessons from your errors and the general willingness to learn. Every revolutionary organization and every guerrilla organization knows that practice requires that it develop its capabilities—at least any organization applying dialectical materialism, any organization that aims for victory in the people's war and not the edification of a party bureaucracy and a partnership with imperialist power.

We don't talk about democratic centralism because the urban guerrilla in Germany can't have a centralized apparatus. It is not a party but a politico-military organization within which leadership is exercised collectively within each unit, with a tendency for it to be dissolved as part of the collective learning process. Tactically, the goal is to always

---

6   V.I. Lenin, "Imperialism and the Split in Socialism," in *Collected Works*, vol. 23 (Moscow: Progress Publishers, 1964), 119–20.

7   Le Duan, "Principles and Methods of Revolutionary Action," in *The Vietnamese Revolution: Fundamental Problems and Essential Tasks* (New York: International Publishers, 1971). Le Duan was one of the founders of the Vietnamese Communist Party, its chairman, and Ho Chi Minh's successor.

8   Karl Marx, "The Eighteenth Brumaire of Louis Napoleon," in *Marx and Engels Collected Works*, vol. 11 (London: Lawrence & Wishart, 1975), 107.

allow for an autonomous orientation toward militants, guerrillas, and cadres. Collectivity is a political process that functions on all levels: in interaction and communication and in the sharing of knowledge that occurs as we work and learn together. An authoritarian leadership structure would find no material basis in the guerrilla, because the real (i.e., voluntary) development of each individual's productive force is necessary for the revolutionary guerrilla to make an effective revolutionary intervention from a position of weakness, in order to launch the people's liberation war.

Psychological Warfare

Andreas, because he is a revolutionary, and was one from the beginning, is the primary target of the psychological war that the cops are waging against us. This has been the case since 1970, since the first appearance of the urban guerrilla with the prison break operation.

The guiding principle of psychological warfare is to set the people against the guerrilla, to isolate the guerrilla from the people, to distort the real, material goals of the revolution by personalizing events and by presenting them in psychological terms. The goals of the revolution are freedom from imperialist domination, from occupation, from colonialism and neocolonialism, from the dictatorship of the bourgeoisie, from military dictatorship, from exploitation, from fascism, and from imperialism. Psychological warfare uses the tactic of mystifying that which is easy enough to understand, presenting as irrational that which is rational, and presenting the revolutionaries' humanity as inhumanity. This is carried out by means of defamation, lies, insults, bullshit, racism, manipulation, and the mobilization of the people's unconscious fears and reflexes inculcated over decades and centuries of colonial domination and exploitation—knee-jerk existential fear in the face of incomprehensible and hidden powers of domination.

Through psychological warfare, the cops attempt to eliminate revolutionary politics and the armed anti-imperialist struggle in Germany, as well as its effect on the consciousness of the people, by personalizing it and turning it into a psychological issue. In this way, the cops attempt to present us as what they themselves are, they attempt to present the RAF's structure as similar to their own, a structure of domination mimicking the organizational form and functioning of their own structures of domination, a structure like that of the Ku Klux Klan, the mafia, the CIA. And they accuse us of the tactics that imperialism and its puppets use to impose themselves: extortion, corruption, competition, privilege, brutality, paving the road with corpses.

In their use of psychological warfare against us, the cops rely upon the confusion of all those who are obliged to sell their labor simply to survive, a confusion born of the obligation to produce and of the fear for one's very existence that the system generates within them. They rely on the morbid practice of defamation, which the ruling class has directed against the people for decades, for centuries; a mixture of anticommunism, antisemitism, racism, sexual oppression, religious oppression, and an authoritarian educational system. They rely on consumer society brainwashing and the imperialist media, re-education and the "economic miracle."

What is shocking about the guerrilla in its first phase, what was shocking about its first actions, is that they showed that people could act outside of the system's limits, that they didn't have to see through the media's eyes, that they could be free from fear—that people could act on the basis of their own very real experiences, their own and those of the people. Because the guerrilla starts from the fact that—despite this country's highly advanced technology and immense wealth—every day people have their own experiences with oppression, media terrorism, and insecure living conditions, leading to mental illness, suicide, child abuse, indoctrination, and housing shortages. That is what the imperialist state finds shocking about our actions: that the people can understand the RAF for what it is: a practice, a cause born in a logical and dialectical way from actual relationships. A practice which—insofar as it is the expression of real relationships, insofar as it expresses the only real possibility for reversing and changing these relationships—gives the people their dignity and makes sense out of struggle, revolution, uprisings, defeats, and past revolts—that is to say, it returns to the people the possibility of being conscious of their own history. Because all history is the history of class struggle, a people who has lost a sense of the significance of revolutionary class struggle is forced to live in a state in which they no longer participate in history, in which they are deprived of their sense of self, that is to say, of their dignity.

In the guerrilla, everyone can determine for themselves where they stand, can find, often for the first time, their place in class society, in imperialism, can make these decisions for themselves. Many people think they are on the side of the people, but the moment the people start to confront the police and start to fight, they cut and run, issue denunciations, put the brakes on, and side with the police. This is a problem that Marx often addressed: that one is not what one believes oneself to be but what one is in one's true functions, in one's role within class society. That is to say, if one doesn't decide to act against the system, doesn't take up arms and fight, then one is on the system's side and effectively serves as an instrument for achieving the system's goals.

With psychological warfare, the cops attempt to turn the achievements of the guerrilla's actions back against us: the knowledge that it isn't the people who are dependent on the state but the state that is dependent on the people—that it isn't the people who need the investment firms or the multinationals and their factories, but it is the capitalist pigs who need the people—that the goal of the police isn't to protect the people from criminals but to protect the imperialist order of exploitation from the people—that the people don't need the justice system, but the justice system needs the people—that we don't need the American troops and installations here, but that US imperialism needs us. Through personalization and psychological rationalization, they project the clichés of capitalist anthropology onto us. They project the reality of their own facade, of their judges, of their prosecutors, of their screws, and of their fascists, pigs who take pleasure in their alienation, who only live by torturing, by oppressing, and by exploiting others, pigs for whom the whole point of their existence is their career, success, elbowing their way to the top, and taking advantage of others, pigs who take pleasure from the hunger, the misery, and the deprivation of millions of human beings in the Third World and here.

What the ruling class hates about us is that despite a hundred years of repression, of fascism, of anticommunism, of imperialist wars, and of genocides, the revolution once again raises its head. In carrying out psychological warfare, the bourgeoisie, with its police state, sees in us everything that they hate and fear about the people, and this is especially so in the case of Andreas. It is he who is the mob, the street, the enemy. They see in us that which menaces them and will overthrow them: the determination to provoke the revolution, revolutionary violence, and political and military action. At the same time they see their own powerlessness, for their power ends at the point when the people take up arms and begin to struggle.

The system is exposing itself, not us, in its defamation campaign. All defamation campaigns against the guerrilla reveal something about those who carry them out, about their fat bellies, their goals, their ambitions, and their fears.

And to say we are "a vanguard that designates itself as such" makes no sense. To be the vanguard is a role that we cannot assign ourselves, nor is it one that we can demand. It is a role that the people give to the guerrilla in their own consciousness, in the process of developing their consciousness, of rediscovering their role in history as they recognize themselves in the guerrilla's actions, because they, "in themselves," recognize the necessity to destroy the system "for themselves" through guerrilla actions. The idea of a "vanguard that designates itself as such" reflects ideas of prestige that belong to a ruling class that seeks to dominate. But that has nothing to do with the role of the proletariat, a role that is based on the absence of property, on emancipation, on dialectical materialism, and on the struggle against imperialism.

The Dialectic of Revolution and Counterrevolution

That is the dialectic of the anti-imperialist struggle. The enemy unmasks itself by its defensive maneuvers, by the system's reaction, by the counterrevolutionary escalation, by the transformation of the political state of emergency into a military state of emergency. This is how it shows its true face—and by its terrorism it provokes the masses to rise up against it, reinforcing the contradictions and making revolution inevitable.

As Marighella said:

> The basic principle of revolutionary strategy in conditions of permanent political crisis is to develop, in the city as well as in the countryside, such a breadth of revolutionary activity that the enemy finds himself obliged to transform the political situation in the country into a military situation. In this way dissatisfaction spreads to all layers of the population, with the military alone responsible for all of the hatred.[9]

---

9   ALN, "Problems and Principles of Strategy," in Carlos Marighella, *For the Liberation of Brazil* (Harmondsworth, UK: Penguin Books, 1971), 46.

And as a Persian comrade, A.P. Puyan, said:

> By extending the violence against the resistance fighters, creating an unanticipated reaction, the repression inevitably hits all other oppressed milieus and classes in an even more massive way. As a result, the ruling class augments the contradictions between the oppressed classes and itself and creates a climate which leads of necessity to a great leap forward in the consciousness of the masses.[10]

And Marx said:

> Revolutionary progress breaks ground by the creation of a powerful, united counterrevolution, by the creation of an opponent in combat with whom alone the party of insurrection ripen[s] into a really revolutionary party.[11]

In 1972, the cops mobilized 150,000 men to hunt the RAF, using television to involve the people in the manhunt, having the federal chancellor intervene, and centralizing all police forces in the hands of the BKA. This makes it clear that, already at that point, a numerically insignificant group of revolutionaries was all it took to set in motion all of the material and human resources of the state. It was already clear that the state's monopoly of violence had material limits, that their forces could be exhausted, that if, on the tactical level, imperialism is a beast that devours humans, on the strategic level it is a paper tiger. It was clear that it is up to us whether the oppression continues, and it is also up to us to smash it.

Now, after everything they have carried out against us with their psychological warfare campaign, the pigs are preparing to assassinate Andreas. As of today, we political prisoners, members of the RAF and other anti-imperialist groups, are beginning a hunger strike. We must add the fact that for some years now—in keeping with the police

---

10   Amir-Parviz Puyan, *The Necessity of Armed Struggle and Refutation of the Theory of "Survival"* (New York: Support Committee for the Iranian People's Struggle, 1975), 28. Puyan was a founding member of the Organization of the People's Fedayeen Guerrillas, a Marxist-Leninist guerrilla group established in 1971. By the time of the Shah of Iran's overthrow in 1979, it was the most significant guerrilla group operating in Iran.

11   Karl Marx, "The Class Struggles in France, 1948 to 1950," in *Marx and Engels Collected Works*, vol. 10 (London: Lawrence & Wishart, 1975), 47.

objective of liquidating the RAF, and consistent with their tactic of psychological warfare—most of us have found ourselves detained in isolation. Which is to say, we have found ourselves in the process of being exterminated. But we have decided not to stop thinking and struggling; we have decided to dump the rocks the state has thrown at us at its own feet.

The police are preparing to assassinate Andreas, as they attempted previously during the summer 1973 hunger strike when they deprived him of water. At that time, they attempted to have the lawyers and the public believe that he was allowed to drink again after a few days; in reality he received nothing, and the pig of a doctor at the Schwalmstadt prison, after nine days, when he had already gone blind, said, "If you don't drink some milk, you'll be dead in ten hours."[12] The Hesse minister of justice came from time to time to have a look in his cell, and the Hesse prison doctors' group was at that time meeting with the Wiesbaden minister of justice. There exists a decree in Hesse that anticipates breaking hunger strikes by withholding all liquids. The complaints filed against the pig of a doctor for attempted murder were rejected, and the procedure undertaken to maintain the complaint was suspended.

We declare today that if the cops attempt to follow through with their plans to deprive Andreas of water, all prisoners from the RAF participating in the hunger strike will immediately react in turn by refusing all liquids. We will react in the same way if faced with any attempted assassination through the withholding of water, no matter where it occurs or against which prisoner it is used.

---

12 Schwalmstadt, in the federal state of Hesse (capital: Wiesbaden), was the prison where Andreas Baader was held before being transferred to Stammheim prison in Stuttgart in November 1974.

Interview During the Hunger Strike

Interview with Andreas Baader, Gudrun Ensslin, Ulrike Meinhof, and Jan Raspe, published in the news weekly Der Spiegel *on January 20, 1975. The interview was conducted by correspondence with the prisoners in Stammheim in December 1974, during the political prisoners' hunger strike that lasted from September 13, 1974, to February 5, 1975, in the context of which Holger Meins had died on November 9, 1974. Later, the prisoners thought that the circumstances under which the text came about had resulted in an inadequately abbreviated account of the history of the RAF's struggle. However, in our view, the aggressive tone of the text accurately captures the situation of the prisoners and the political context at the time. We have included some corrections that Jan and Gudrun made to their respective copies in preparation of planned book publications in the Summer of 1977.*

Has the RAF adopted a new tactic? Have the campaigns that you prepared and led from within the prisons attracted the same interest among the people as the bombs and grenades you used in 1972?
It is not a matter of empty talk about tactics. We are prisoners, and we are currently struggling with the only weapon we have left in prison and in isolation: the collective hunger strike. We are doing this in order to break through the process of destruction in which we find ourselves—long years of social isolation. It is a life and death struggle: if we don't succeed with this hunger strike, we will either die or be psychologically and physically destroyed by brainwashing, isolation, and special measures.

Is it really a matter of "isolation torture" or even "destruction through prison conditions"? You read a lot of newspapers; if you like you can listen to the radio or watch television. For example, at one point Herr Baader had a library of four hundred books. You are in contact with other members of the RAF. You exchange secret messages among yourselves. You receive visits, and your lawyers come and go.

If one only has access to *Spiegel* or state security information, one might think so. Two, three, four years of social isolation is enough to realize that you are in a process of destruction. You can deal with it for a few months, but not years. Breaking through the institutional brainwashing-by-isolation is a question of survival for us; this is the reason why the trials will go on without us. To claim that we are using the hunger strikes to make ourselves unfit for prison or unfit to appear in court—when everyone knows that the only political prisoners who are considered unfit for prison are those who are dead—is a countertactic; it is counterpropaganda. The AGO has already postponed these trials for three-and-a-half years, so that the prisoners could be broken by isolation, by silent wings, by brainwashing and psychiatric constructs. The AGO is no longer interested in these trials taking place. Or, if they are to take place, it should only be without the accused and without their defense attorneys, because these are meant to be show trials to discredit revolutionary politics—imperialist state power is to be put on display, and Buback can only achieve this if we are not there.[1]

Such lies don't become more convincing, no matter how many times you repeat them; and the public understood long ago that these lies are put out in bad faith in order to sow doubts about the justice system, a goal in which you have achieved some success.

Because these are facts, whose political relevance cannot be eliminated by simply denying them.

You are being held in remand, having been charged with serious crimes, including murder and attempted murder. Aren't you being held in the same conditions as other prisoners in remand?

---

1   Siegfried Buback was Germany's attorney general. He was killed by a RAF commando on April 7, 1977.

We are demanding an end to the special measures, and not only for those in remand, but for all political prisoners—and by this we mean all proletarian prisoners who understand their situation politically, and who organize in solidarity with the prisoners' struggle, regardless of why they are in prison.

The justice system also keeps prisoners who have already been sentenced in isolation, some for as many as four years: for example, Werner Hoppe, Helmut Pohl, Rolf Heißler, Ulrich Luther, and Siegfried Knutz. There are thousands of people here who are abused by the prison system, and the moment they begin to resist they are broken by isolation. This is what we are fighting against with this strike; it is a collective action against the institutionalization of isolation. In the older prisons, where previously there were no isolation facilities—separate wings for "troublemakers"—meaning for those who disrupt the inhumanity which victimizes them—they will be built: for instance, in Tegel, Bruchsal, Straubing, Hannover, Zweibrücken, etc.

In their architectural design, the new prisons incorporate isolation as a form of incarceration. In West Germany, these design principles are not in line with the Swedish model but, rather, with US methods and experiments with fascist rehabilitation programs.

In concrete terms, tell us what you mean by special measures. We have looked into the actual prison conditions of the RAF collective. We found no evidence of "special measures," other than a series of privileges. You have not looked into anything. You got your information from the state security services and the federal prosecution.

When we say special measures, we are referring to:
- eight months in a silent wing for Ulrike and Astrid;
- years of isolation for all the prisoners from the RAF;
- forced anesthesia ordered by the court "for identification purposes";
- years of being handcuffed during yard time;
- ongoing court-ordered "immediate use of force," which means cruel treatment in pacification cells, during transportation, during interrogations, during identification line ups, and during visits;
- newspaper censorship;
- special legislation;

- special buildings for the trials of prisoners from the RAF in Kaiserslautern and in Stammheim—the 150 million DM bloated state security budget for the Stammheim trial to take place in a concrete fortress, which will require the relocation of police units from three federal states, even though it looks like neither the accused nor their lawyers will even be allowed to be present—assuming, that is, that the justice system lets the accused live that long;
- obstruction of the defense, publication of defense materials, files, and state security documents and using them in government campaigns to determine the verdicts and have the defense barred.

The Springer press has access to defense files and to files that the AGO has withheld from the defense. The defense attorneys are watched day and night. Their mail is opened, their telephones are bugged, and their offices are searched. They receive disciplinary sanctions from the bar for their public work. Relatives and visitors are harassed by the state security services, even at their jobs. They have been terrorized with open surveillance. Anyone who wants to write to us or visit us is spied on and ends up in the state security services' files.

Because of the pressure from the hunger strike, they have made cosmetic changes, small things, details, which the Ministry presents to film crews. In reality, nothing has changed.

The reality right now is that isolation is organized within the prisons with deadly technical precision—now with prisoners allowed to be together in groups of two for a few hours at a time. This doesn't interfere with the destructive process; it remains a closed system. This means that the brainwashing is to continue and any social interaction will remain impossible. In regards to the outside, isolation is perfected by excluding the lawyers or else by limiting their number to three at a time.

Given Posser's conditions[2]—for example, our six years of remand—and the role of the AGO in postponing the trial, it's clear what we mean by "destruction through prison conditions." Disprove even one of these "privileges"!

---

2   Diether Posser, minister of justice for the federal state of North Rhine-Westphalia.

First you said that force-feeding was a fascist tactic; then, after Holger Meins died of starvation, you described his death as a "murder by installment." Isn't that a contradiction?

We're not the ones who said that, but force-feeding is a tactic used to diminish the effect of the hunger strike—how it appears—on the outside world; in short, to camouflage the murder. This is why intensive care units were set up in the prisons, so that it could be said that "they did everything they could," although they didn't do the simplest thing they could have done: abolish isolation and special measures.

Holger Meins was intentionally executed by systematic undernourishment. From the beginning, force-feeding in Wittlich prison was a method of assassination. At first, it was carried out by brutal and direct violence to break his will. After that, it was only done for show. With four hundred calories a day, it is only a matter of time, certainly only days, before one dies. Buback and the BKA's Security Group arranged for Holger Meins to remain in Wittlich prison until he died. On October 21 [1974], the Stuttgart Supreme Court ordered that Holger Meins be transferred to Stuttgart by November 2 at the latest. On October 24, Buback informed the Stuttgart court that the Security Group would not be able to respect this timetable—a fact that was only made public after Holger's death. Finally, Hutter, the prison doctor, completely cut off the force-feeding and went on vacation.

It must also be pointed out that throughout the hunger strike the BKA received "reports" from the prison administration as to the prisoners' condition.[3] It must be emphasized that in an effort to protect himself, because he could see that Holger was dying, before Hutter left he asked Degenhardt to guarantee that he would not face charges, in the same way that all of the charges against Degenhardt had been dropped. Degenhardt was the doctor in Schwalmstadt who, in the summer of 1973, during the second hunger strike, cut off water for nine days "for medical reasons," until Andreas fell into a coma.[4] He is the doctor who Buback

---

3   The BKA is Germany's federal investigation bureau, akin to the US FBI. The BKA's Security Group (Sicherungsgruppe Bonn) was the predecessor of the BKA's Terrorism Department (BKA-TE). This unit was responsible for both the hunt for RAF members and for determining the transport and detention conditions of the prisoners from the RAF.

4   Schwalmstadt was the prison where Andreas Baader was kept until his transfer to Stammheim prison in Stuttgart in November 1974. During the first two hunger strikes

described to Frey, who was dealing with the prisoners in Zweibrücken, as having what it takes.

Holger was assassinated according to a plan by which the scheduling of his transfer was manipulated to create an opening that the AGO and the Security Group could use to target the prisoner directly. The fact that so far no journalist has looked into this and nobody has written about it doesn't change the facts, but it does say everything that needs to be said about the collaboration, complicity, and personal ties between the media conglomerates and state security: the AGO, the BKA, and the intelligence services.

There is no way we can accept your version of the so-called "murder by installment" of Meins. It seems to us that you have a persecution complex, which would make sense after years spent underground and in prison. We at Der Spiegel *criticized Dr. Hutter's behavior, and the AGO launched an investigation into his actions.*
It's not about Hutter or any other prison doctor—they decide practically nothing. The medical system in prison is organized hierarchically, and at most Hutter is an expendable figure. He's a pig, but only a little one, who in the long run might be held accountable, although nobody who knows anything about prison or prison medicine would believe it. When you say you "criticized" him, you are referring to the old trick of talking about "mistakes," so that the actual mistake will not be understood: class society, its justice system, and its prison camps.

Given the situation in the prisons, the media's fascist demagogy around the hunger strike, the chorus of professional politicians—the uncontrollable outburst against a nonviolent action carried out by a small group of people, imprisoned and isolated, who have been forced on the defensive as if the hunger strike were a military attack—Strauß spoke of martial law[5]—all of this shows to what point the system's political and economic crises have eroded its facade of legitimacy. That's where you should look for the sickness, in the state's real interest in destroying the prisoners from the RAF, instead of babbling about persecution complexes.

---

in 1973, Andreas was deprived of water from February 9 to 14 and again from May 24 to June 4.

5   Franz Josef Strauß was the chairman of the Christian Social Union (CSU), the CDU's Bavarian fraternal party.

The British recently stopped the use of force-feeding, for instance, in dealing with the terrorists from the IRA. The hunger strikes stopped right away. How would you react if this was done here?

That's not *our* problem. The CDU calls for an end to force-feeding, in the same way that it leans openly toward a state of emergency and fascism, while the SPD uses its electoral base and its history toward the same end—fascism.[6] State control of every aspect of life, total militarization of politics, media manipulation, and indoctrination of the people, all to promote the domestic and foreign policies of West German imperialism. Public policy amounts to disguising "social shortcomings" and selling them as reforms. So the CDU openly advocates murder, while the SPD passes off the murders as suicides, being unable to openly embrace the state security hard line, which in the final analysis determines our prison conditions.

Isn't this another case of your tilting at windmills? Is it not true that everything we have heard from the RAF so far is based on a patently false analysis of this state, this society, this SPD, this CDU, this justice system?

What you're serving up here is a bit foolish. What you describe as "patently false" cannot be marketed, and our position (proletarian counterpower) is, analytically and practically, antagonistic to yours (imperialist power).

It would be symptomatic of a lack of analysis to talk about the weaknesses, the effects, and the basis of revolutionary politics—which it is your job to dispute—to a journalism that has long asserted openly its support role for the state, and whose negation is proletarian politics. For us, the question—as a question coming from *Der Spiegel*—is pointless. Theory and practice *become* united in the struggle—that's their dialectic. We develop our analysis as a weapon—that way it is concrete, and it has only been presented in cases in which we have control of its publication.

You won't end your hunger strike until your demands have been met. Do you think you have any chance of success? Or will you escalate matters

---

6   The Christian Democratic Union (CDU) is the mainstream conservative party; the Social Democratic Party (SPD) is Germany's mainstream social democratic party.

and, for instance, begin a thirst strike if the demands are not met? What further actions are you preparing inside and outside of prison? Buback still believes that he can break the hunger strike and use it to destroy us by murder, psychological warfare, counterpropaganda—and forced psychiatric treatment, for which intensive-care units are being prepared in the prisons, where we can be strapped down twenty-four hours a day for force-feeding accompanied by psychiatric drugs, so as to keep us in complete physical and mental immobility.

Buback received the help he needed from, among other places, Heinemann's initiative,[7] but also from the precisely worded fascism of the *Der Spiegel* essay written by Ditfurth,[8] for whom murder and forced psychiatric treatment are fair game for his cynical distortions, meant to increase the brutality of the political climate around the hunger strike. When, in mid-November, Carstens began to produce propaganda openly calling for our murder, it still created something like public shock, antagonism, horrified protest, and outrage.[9] It was Heinemann's role to eliminate any lingering doubts—among intellectuals, writers, and the churches—regarding Buback's hard line. It has always been the role of this character to dress up the aggressive policies of West German imperialism in a language and form that makes them seem humane. Heinemann's letters amounted to an appeal for us to submit to brainwashing or murder. In the same way that he, as president, pardoned Ruhland,[10] with his letters he promoted the death sentences the AGO wanted to impose on us, with humanist gestures that soothe the conscience of his supporters. What he wanted was to clear the way for murder—just like in Easter 1968,[11] during his presidency, when he hoped to integrate the students, the old anti-fascists, and the New Left into the new fascism.

We will escalate to a thirst strike. We are not planning actions inside or outside of prison, because we are imprisoned and isolated.

---

7   Gustav Heinemann, representative of the radical democratic wing of German Protestantism. After a period of political wandering, he was an SPD member of the federal parliament from 1957 to 1969, minister of justice from 1966 to 1969, and president of the republic from 1969 to 1974. In two open letters he appealed to Ulrike to end the hunger strike.

8   Christian von Ditfurth, journalist.

9   Karl Carstens, then leader of the CDU opposition in the federal parliament.

10   Karl-Heinz Ruhland, one of the first witnesses to testify against members of the RAF.

11   Easter 1968 refers to the "Easter riots" after the attempted assassination of student movement spokesperson Rudi Dutschke in April 1968.

Did Holger Meins's death provide the RAF collective with an opportunity?
That is fascist projection, an idea of someone who can no longer think
except in the terms of the market—the system that reduces all human
life to money, egotism, power, and one's career. Like Che, we say, "The
guerrilla should only risk his life if this is absolutely necessary, but
in such a case, without a moment's hesitation." Holger's death most
certainly has "the resonance of history," meaning that what started with
the armed anti-imperialist struggle has become a part of the history of
the people of the world.

"An opportunity" in this case could only mean that it broke through
the news blackout about the strike. You yourself bear some responsibility for the fact that lots of people only woke up when someone was
finally murdered and only then began to realize what was going on. For
eight weeks *Der Spiegel* did not say a word about the hunger strike of
forty political prisoners, in order to prevent solidarity and protection.
Your first report on it appeared on the fifty-third day of the strike, five
days before Holger's death.

Are you prepared to see other people die?
Buback is sitting at his desk waiting for that.

You must know that we think that's a monstrous suggestion.
Oestreicher, the Chairman of Amnesty England, a professional human
rights activist, following a conversation with Buback in his efforts at
mediation with the state, was "shocked" by the "ice-cold" way that
Buback "was gambling with the prisoners' lives." That's a quote.

How do you analyze the situation of the Federal Republic of Germany?
An imperialist center. A US colony. A US military base. The leading
imperialist power in Western Europe and in the European Community.
Second strongest military power in NATO. The representative of US
imperialist interests in Western Europe.

The position of West Germany vis à vis the Third World is characterized by the fusion of West German and US imperialism (politically,
economically, militarily, and ideologically, based on the same interests
in exploiting the Third World, as well as on the standardization of their
social structures through the concentration of capital and consumer
culture): in terms of its participation in imperialist wars, as well as being

a "city" in the worldwide revolutionary process of "the encirclement of cities by the rural areas" (Lin Biao).

So the guerrilla in the capitalist centers is an urban guerrilla in both senses: geographically, it emerges, operates, and develops in the big cities, and, strategically, in the politico-military sense, because it attacks imperialism's repressive machinery within the capitalist centers, from the inside, like partisans operating behind enemy lines. That is what we mean by proletarian internationalism today.

To sum up: West Germany is part of US imperialism's system of states, not as an oppressed but as an oppressor state.

In a state like this, the development of proletarian counterpower and the liberation struggle to disrupt the ruling power structure must be internationalist right from the beginning, which is only possible through a strategic and tactical relationship with the liberation struggles of the oppressed nations.

Historically, since 1918–1919, the German imperialist bourgeoisie and its state have held the initiative in an offensive against the people, from the complete destruction of the proletariat's organizations under fascism, through the defeat of the old fascism, not by armed struggle here, but by the Soviet army and the Western Allies, and onward up until today.

In the 1920s, there was the economic fatalism of the Third International,[12] with the communist parties totally aligned with the Soviet Union, which prevented the KPD from advancing the revolution and conquering power through a policy oriented around armed struggle, through which it could have developed a class identity and revolutionary energy. After 1945, US imperialism tried to brainwash the people with anticommunism, consumer culture, and the political, ideological, and even military restoration of fascism in the form of the Cold War. Nor did East Germany present communist politics as a liberation struggle. Unlike France, Italy, Yugoslavia, Greece, Spain, and even Holland, the antifascist resistance here hasn't been acknowledged by the population. What was left of it after 1945 was immediately destroyed by the Western Allies.

---

12   See also the statements at the Stammheim trial about the history of Germany and the Third International (pp. 106–11, this volume).

What this means for us and for the legal left here is that we don't have much to hold on to, nothing to base ourselves on historically, nothing that we can take for granted in terms of proletarian organization or consciousness, not even democratic republican traditions. In terms of domestic policies, this is one of the factors which makes the drift toward fascism possible, with the exaggerated runaway growth of the police apparatus, the state security machine as a state within the state, the de facto concentration of power, and the proliferation of special legislation in the framework of "internal security"—from the emergency laws to the current special laws that allow show trials to be held in the absence of the accused and their lawyers, permit the exclusion of "radicals" from the public service, and extend the jurisdiction of the BKA. A democracy that is not won by the people but is imposed on them has no mass base, cannot be defended, and won't be.

All this sums up the specific conditions of the political terrain of West Germany.

So far, all of your bombs and slogans have only attracted very small groups of intellectuals and anarchist fellow travelers. Do you think you'll be able to change this?
The Third World peoples' liberation wars have economic, political, military, and ideological repercussions within society in the capitalist centers, which Lin Biao referred to as "cutting the feet out from under imperialism." They accentuate the contradictions within the capitalist centers. The techniques the system depends on to cover up these contradictions cease to work. Reform turns into repression. In areas where people lack social necessities, the military and police budgets are enormously bloated. Inevitably, the system's crisis unfolds: impoverishment of the people, militarization of politics, and increased repression. To intervene, from the historic and political defensive, in this process of disintegration forms the basis for any revolutionary politics here.

You are often criticized for having absolutely no influence on the masses or connections to a political base. Do you think this might be because the RAF collective is out of touch with reality? Have you sharpened your perspective? Many now feel that the only people paying attention to you are those who feel sorry for you, and that even the far left does not approve of you. Where do you think your supporters are?

There is the *trace* of the RAF's politics. Not supporters, fellow travelers, or successor organizations, but the RAF and the political effect of our politics—to the degree that—as a result of the measures the government has taken against us—many people are seeing this state for what it is: the repressive tool of the imperialist bourgeoisie against the people. To the degree that they identify with our struggle, they will become conscious—the system's power will eventually show itself to be relative, not absolute. They will discover that one can do something, that the feeling of powerlessness does not reflect objective reality on the level of proletarian internationalism. They will become conscious of the connection between the liberation struggles in the Third World and here, conscious of the need to cooperate and work together legally and illegally. On the level of practice: that it's not enough to talk, that it is both possible and necessary to act.

Do you intend to remain a cadre organization and bring down the system all by yourselves or do you still think you will be able to mobilize the proletarian masses?
No revolutionary wants to "bring down the system on their own," that's ridiculous. There is no revolution without the people. Things like this have been said about Blanqui, Lenin, Che, and now they say it about us, but they only ever say this to denounce revolutionary initiative, appealing to the masses in order to justify and sell reformist politics.

It is not a matter of struggling alone but of creating, out of the everyday struggles, mobilizations, and organizing on the part of the legal left, a politico-*military* core that can establish an illegal infrastructure, which is necessary in order to be able to act. In conditions of persecution, an illegal practice must be developed to provide continuity, orientation, strength, and direction to the legal struggles in the factories, the neighborhoods, the streets, and the universities, commensurate with the degree of development of the imperialist system's economic and political crisis: conquering *political* power.

Our political objective, what we are struggling to develop, is a strong guerrilla movement in the capitalist centers. This is a necessary step, in this phase of US imperialism's definite defeat and decline, if the legal movements and the movements that develop in response to the system's contradictions are not to be destroyed as soon as they appear. In this age of multinational capital, of transnational imperialist repression at home and abroad, the guerrilla organizes proletarian counterpower, and in so doing represents the same thing as the Bolshevik cadre party did in Lenin's days. It will develop through this process—nationally and internationally—into a revolutionary party.

It is stupid to say that we are acting alone, given the actual state of anti-imperialist struggles in Asia, Latin America, and Africa, in Vietnam, Chile, Uruguay, Argentina, and Palestine. The RAF is not alone in Western Europe: there is also the IRA, the ETA, and the armed groups in Italy, Portugal, and England. There have been urban guerrilla groups in North America since 1968.

It seems that right now your base consists of forty RAF comrades in prison and about three hundred anarchists living underground in West Germany. What about your sympathizer scene?
Those are the constantly-changing numbers issued by the BKA. They are incorrect. It is not so simple to quantify the process by which people become conscious. At the moment solidarity is spreading internationally. At the same time, international public opinion is becoming increasingly aware of West German imperialism and of the repression that goes on here.

Throughout the RAF's existence, there has been an increasing process of discussion and polarization on the legal left regarding the question of armed struggle. A new antifascism is taking shape, one which is not based on the apolitical pity for the victims and the persecuted but on an identification with the anti-imperialist struggle, directed against the police, the state security services, the multinational corporations, US imperialism.

Helmut Schmidt wouldn't have listed the RAF in his New Year's speech under the five facts/developments that are most threatening to imperialism in 1974[13]—worldwide inflation, the oil crisis, Guillaume,[14] unemployment, and the RAF—if we were fish out of water, if revolutionary politics here had as limited a base as you and the psychological warfare campaigns claim.

---

13   Helmut Schmidt (SPD), chancellor of West Germany from 1974 to 1982.
14   Günter Guillaume, an East German spy on the staff of Chancellor Willy Brandt (SPD), Helmut Schmidt's predecessor, was one of the reasons that Brandt was forced to step down.

It is said that one of your main sources of support is the dozen or so lawyers who are in charge of coordinating things for you inside and outside of the prisons. What role do your lawyers play?
That of committed lawyers. Lawyers who are involved in our cases are inevitably politicized, because quite literally at every turn, right from their very first visit with a prisoner from the RAF, they experience the fact that nothing they took for granted about the legal system holds true. The body searches, the mail censorship, the cell raids, the hysteria, the paranoia, the disciplinary committee rulings, the criminalization, the psychological warfare, the legislation custom-made to exclude them, on top of what they see of the special conditions we are subjected to, and their utter powerlessness to change anything in the normal way, that is to say, by using legal arguments in court, and the fact that every step of the way they see that it is not the judges who are making the decisions regarding us, but the BKA's Security Group and the AGO. The discrepancy between the letter of the law and the reality of the law, between the pretense of the rule of law and the reality of a police state, turns them into defenders of the constitutional state, into anti-fascists.

It is part of the counterstrategy of the AGO and the BKA to claim that these lawyers are our "auxiliary forces," which they are not. To a large degree, the justice system has been taken over by state security, in order to serve the goals of the counterinsurgency campaign and to aid in the AGO's extermination strategy. In this context, defense attorneys who insist on the separation of powers are considered obstacles to the drift toward fascism and must inevitably be targeted.

Do you have political disagreements with other underground anarchist groups?
Not in an interview with *Der Spiegel*.

What about the 2nd of June Movement, which murdered the West Berlin Supreme Court Judge Drenkmann?[15]
Ask the 2nd of June Movement.

---

15 Günter von Drenkmann, president of the West Berlin Court of Appeal, killed by the 2nd of June Movement during an attempted kidnapping in response to Holger Meins's death and in support of the hunger strike.

What do you think? Did Drenkmann's murder accomplish anything?
Drenkmann didn't become the top judge in a city of almost three
million without ruining the lives of thousands of people, depriving
them of their right to life, choking them with laws, locking them away
in prison cells, destroying their futures.

What's more, despite calls from the highest West German authorities, the president of the republic and the president of the constitutional
court, only fifteen thousand Berliners came out to the funeral, and this
in a city where five to six hundred thousand people used to come out
for anticommunist demonstrations. You yourselves know that all the
indignation about this attack on the Berlin judge is nothing but propaganda and hypocrisy; nobody mourns a character mask. This whole
exercise was just a way for the bourgeoisie and the imperialists to send
a message. The indignation was just a reflex action in one particular
political climate, nothing more.

Those who, without themselves being from the ruling elite, identify
with such a character mask of the justice system simply make it clear
that wherever exploitation reigns, they can only imagine themselves on
the side of the exploiter. In terms of class analysis, leftists and liberals
who protested the Drenkmann action simply exposed themselves.

*We know something quite different. We know that Drenkmann was
shot, and we consider the RAF s justification of this murder to be outrageous, nothing but lynch mob justice for a so-called "crime" that was
committed collectively by what you refer to as a "fascist" justice system.
Even if one accepts the maxim that the ends justify the means, as you
obviously do, one can see by the public's reaction that Drenkmann's
murder constituted a setback for the RAF.*
The logic behind the means lies with the ends. We are not justifying
anything. Revolutionary counterviolence is not only legitimate, it is our
only option, and we expect that as it develops it will give the class that
you write for many more opportunities to offer up ignorant opinions,
and not just about the attempted kidnapping of a judge. The action
was powerful—as an expression of our love and our mourning and
rage about the murder of an imprisoned combatant. If there are to be
funerals—then they will be on both sides.

Your indignation has to be seen in the light of your silence regarding the attack in Bremen, where a bomb went off in a locker shortly

after a football game had been cancelled. Unlike the action against Drenkmann, this bomb was not aimed at a member of the ruling class but at the people; it was a CIA-style fascist action, and it met with a much less heated reaction. How do you explain that in this case the Bremen Railway Police were already on alert the morning of December 8 [1974]—the day that the bomb went off at 4:15 p.m.—because they had been warned by the Hesse state police to expect an attack in the station or on a train. How do you explain the fact that at 3:30 p.m. the Civil Protection Service in Bremen-North had already received the order to send five ambulances to the central station because a bomb was going to explode, while the police, who were there immediately after the explosion, claimed that they had only received word of the bomb threat at 3:56 pm, and that they had thought it was going to go off in a downtown department store? The Bremen authorities not only knew the exact time and place of this attack, but immediately afterwards they had this statement prepared to conceal, manipulate, and deflect any investigation away from what they had actually been doing. So where is your indignation there?[16]

We will look into your allegations. While underground, you yourselves emphasized violence. When the bombs went off in Munich, Heidelberg, and Hamburg, the RAF saw these as political acts and claimed them as such. Since then have you recognized that violence against property and people is ineffective—that it doesn't attract solidarity but, rather, repels it—or do you intend to continue along this path?

The question is: Who does it repel? Our photos were hung in the streets of Hanoi, because the RAF attack in Heidelberg destroyed the computer that was used to program and guide US bomber deployments against North Vietnam. The US officers and soldiers and politicians found this repellent, because, in Frankfurt and in Heidelberg, they were suddenly reminded of Vietnam and could no longer feel safe in their hinterland.

Today revolutionary politics must be both political and military. This is a given because of the structure of imperialism, which must guarantee its sphere of control both internally and externally, in its centers and in the Third World, primarily by military means, through military pacts, military interventions, and counterinsurgency programs,

---

16   See Moncourt and Smith, 349 and 371.

and through "internal security," i.e., building up the internal machinery for maintaining power. Given imperialism's capacity for violence, there can be no revolutionary politics without resolving the question of violence at each stage of revolutionary organization.

How do you see yourselves? Do you consider yourselves to be anarchists or Marxists?
Marxists. But the state security image of anarchists is nothing more than an anticommunist hate campaign aimed at portraying anarchists as only being interested in blowing stuff up. In this way, the necessary terminology is established for the government's counterinsurgency campaign, meant to manipulate those anxieties which are always lurking just below the surface. Anxieties about unemployment, crisis, and war, which feed the insecurity about living conditions that people experience in a capitalist society, and which are used to sell the people "internal security" measures as peace and security measures in the form of the state's military machine—the police, the intelligence services, and the army. It aims at a reactionary, fascist mass mobilization of the people, thereby manipulating them into identifying with the state's machinery of violence.

It is also an attempt to turn the old quarrel between Marxism and revolutionary anarchism to the advantage of the imperialist state, to use the contemporary dumbing-down of Marxism against us: "Marxists don't attack the state, they attack capital" and "It is not the streets, but the factories that are key to class struggle" and so on. Given this false understanding of Marxism, Lenin must have been an anarchist, and his work *The State and Revolution* must have been an anarchist work. Whereas it is, in fact, *the* strategic text of revolutionary Marxism. The experience of all the guerrilla movements is simply that the instruments of Marxism-Leninism, that which Lenin, Mao, Giap, Fanon, and Che took from Marxist theory and conveyed from it, was useful for them, a weapon in the anti-imperialist struggle.

So far as the people are concerned, it would seem that the "people's war" as conceived of by the RAF has become a war against the people. Böll once spoke of six against sixty million.[17]

---

17   Heinrich Böll, German novelist.

That's just the wishful thinking of imperialists. In the same way that in 1972 the newspaper *Bild* turned the idea of people's war into "a war against the people." If you think that *Bild* is the voice of the people... We don't share Böll's contempt for the masses, because NATO, the multinational corporations, state security, the 127 US military bases in West Germany, Dow Chemical, IBM, General Motors, the justice system, the police, and the BGS are not the people. Furthermore, hammering into the people's consciousness the idea that the policies of the oil companies, the CIA, the BND, the VS, and the BKA[18] are in the interests of the people and that the imperialist state represents the common good is the function of *Bild*, *Der Spiegel*, and the psychological war waged by state security against the people and against us.

Vox populi, vox RAF? Haven't you noticed that nobody takes to the streets for you anymore? When there is a RAF trial, hardly anyone shows up in court. Haven't you noticed that from the moment you began throwing bombs nobody has been willing to shelter you? All of which goes some way to explaining the successes in the hunt for the RAF since 1972. It is you and not Böll who have contempt for the people.
It's nice of you to repeat Hacker's clichés,[19] but the situation is this: a tactically weak and divided legal left, facing heavy repression in the national context, cannot transform the reactionary mobilization into one that is revolutionary. It's not even thinkable. In this precise contradiction proletarian politics can become the politics of the proletariat only as armed politics, through transformations that—as problems pertaining to revolution, strategy, class analysis—are certainly beyond the comprehension of your silly polemics.

The RAF, its politics, its line, its actions are proletarian, a beginning of proletarian counterviolence. The struggle has begun. You talk about the fact that some of us are prisoners—that is *one* setback. You don't talk about the political price the imperialist state has paid hunting just one small unit of the RAF. Because one of the goals of revolutionary action—its tactic at this point in its development—is to force the state

---

18   The BGS (Bundesgrenzschutz) is the German border security police. The BKA (Bundeskriminalamt) is the German equivalent of the FBI. The BND (Bundesnachrichtendienst) is the German foreign intelligence service. The VS (Verfassungsschutz) is the German internal intelligence service at both the federal and state levels.

19   Friedrich Hacker, an aspiring psychiatric expert in the areas of aggression and terrorism.

to show itself, to force a reaction from the repressive structure, so that the tools of repression become obvious and can be transformed into the basis for struggle in a revolutionary initiative. Marx said: Revolution progresses "not by its immediate tragicomic achievements but, on the contrary, by the creation of a powerful, united counterrevolution, by the creation of an opponent in combat with whom the party of overthrow ripen[s] into a really revolutionary party."[20]

The surprising thing is not that we suffered a defeat, but that five years later the RAF is still here. The facts to which the government alludes have changed. In answer to a poll in 1972, 20 percent of adults indicated that they would hide one of us at their home for a night, even if it meant risking criminal charges. In 1973, a poll of high schools found that 15 percent of high school students identified with the RAF's actions. Of course, the value of revolutionary politics cannot be measured through opinion polls, as one cannot quantify the processes of becoming conscious, of gaining knowledge, and of becoming politicized, but this does show how the concept of armed insurrection develops into protracted people's war—this shows that through the struggle against the imperialist power structure, the people will eventually recognize their role and will break free from media brainwashing—because our battle is a realistic one, it is a battle against the real enemies of the people, whereas the counterrevolution is obliged to stand facts on their head.

At the same time, there is the problem of chauvinism in people's consciousness in the capitalist centers, which is poorly addressed by the concept of labor aristocracy as an economic category. There is the problem that national identity can only be reactionary in the capitalist centers, where it implies an identification with imperialism. This means that right from the beginning, popular revolutionary consciousness is only possible in the form of proletarian internationalism, by identifying with the anti-imperialist liberation struggles of the people in the Third World. It cannot develop simply through class struggle here. It is the role of the guerrilla in the capitalist centers to create this connection, to make proletarian internationalism the basis for revolutionary politics here, to connect the class struggle here and the liberation struggles of the people of the Third World.

---

20   Karl Marx, "The Class Struggles in France, 1848 to 1850," in *Marx and Engels Selected Works*, vol. 1 (Moscow: Progress Publishers, 1969), 1.

Letter to a Lawyer Regarding the Application of the High Treason Law

This letter mainly addresses Ulrike's view of the prisoners' strategy and the role of the lawyers at the Stammheim trial. One of the special laws introduced for the Stammheim trial forbade lawyers from representing multiple defendants, in order to prevent communication between the prisoners and to make any collective defense more difficult. As such, Ulrike's letter is directed specifically against the individual nature of the defense mandates, i.e., against fragmenting the defense in a way that would prevent lawyers from coordinating with the prisoners and that would limit their involvement to defending only the prisoner they were formally representing in court.

In principle, the thinking of the lawyer addressed here, regarding the request to apply the high treason law, was not entirely absurd. The law had been used by the Nazis against communists to emphasize the political character of the trials against them. In the trials against the RAF, charges and convictions for high treason were rejected by the state security court specifically to depoliticize the trials and thereby claim that they were "completely normal criminal proceedings." In the trials of communists in the 1950s, lawyers sought to invoke the high treason law primarily to show the continuity of anticommunist persecution. As Ulrike points out here, such tactics were rejected by the prisoners from the RAF in the trials against them, because the RAF naturally had a different relationship to the government and the state than had been the case for the KPD.

So you won't be doing that high treason thing—that is, the attempt to use "high treason" as an umbrella term for the charges in the proceedings, because I don't know what you want with it, what you want at all...

High treason followed by an amnesty, as your thinking goes, as an idea, already constitutes a treasonous line, and, concretely, presented by the lawyer who has my mandate, it would amount to an offer to the Attorney General's Office to participate as a lawyer in my destruction. Well, in Stammheim you find yourself on hot terrain, and I am beginning to see that either you get with it or it's not going to work out—at least not with a mandate from me. I am not going along with this.

So either you understand that you have a protective role as our lawyer, or we're going to have to let it go. Prinzing[1]—which means the AGO—is licking his chops at your situation right now. That much is *clear*. They can see that you aren't raising the issue of prison conditions, torture, forced x-rays, or the threat of ether anesthesia,[2] as well as the fact that you have discussions with the court-imposed lawyers.[3] (And again: it's not that "the protocol is so strict here"; it is a matter of your commitment.)

If it is not possible for *you* to refrain from talking to people whose job it is to destroy us, then I forbid you to do so, and if you still don't refrain, you will force me to terminate the mandate. It's as simple as that.

The protocol here is such that we, captured guerrillas, do not accept lawyers who speak to the bureaucrats who are participating in the AGO's extermination strategy, not without purposeful, thoughtful, and discussed intent—that is, without an instruction from us to do so. This isn't paternalism. In this confrontation, it is a necessity: the trial, the prosecution's war against us—counterinsurgency—including against the prisoners from the RAF—so, yes, a thoroughly defensive revolutionary struggle, in which we cannot act alone, in the totally legal context of the prison, cut off from the public, which, besides being intolerable, is indeed another aspect of isolation.

High treason, with speculation about amnesty (which is a justified speculation from all experience: either the death penalty or a pardon), implies that on our side it is a matter of an action aimed at the conquest

---

1   Theodor Prinzing, the presiding judge at the Stammheim trial.
2   In July 1973, the attorney general ordered a scintigraphy of Ulrike Meinhof's brain (for psychiatric or stereotactic procedures) and instructed that she be anesthetized if she did not comply. The order was withdrawn after significant mobilizations in Germany and abroad. In March 1972, Carmen Roll was forcibly anesthetized with ether so that she could be fingerprinted.
3   In trials of RAF members, court-imposed lawyers were supposed to formally defend the accused if their chosen lawyers were excluded or refused to participate.

of *state power*, the seizure of the state apparatus, and the enacting of policies different from those of the government, which is not the case. It implies that by criticizing the prosecution from this perspective we would be legally accountable to a different sort of prosecution, i.e., that this judiciary would be considered competent to judge our actions, i.e., to judge us, which is not the case.

This ascribes a legitimacy to this state that it does not have—it is antagonistic to us. Everything this state does *can* only be deadly for us and, as such, lacks legitimacy; the war that this state is waging against us cannot be legitimized.

The speculation about an amnesty implies that you have not given enough thought to our politics or to anything, given that, on the occasion of the Stockholm action, Schmidt said that our release would have been an "unacceptable test" for this state,[4] and he didn't just mean our release in response to a political action, he meant "at all." So for Schmidt an acquittal would be an "unacceptable test of endurance." (This also clarifies what it means for the defense at Stammheim, but what you say is correct: the trial will remain a "festering wound." Okay, it's just that right now you are proceeding in a way that, if you are not careful, may lead to a pleasant outcome for Prinzing and the AGO.) Speculation about an amnesty undermines the relevance of our politics and downplays the full scope of the state's reaction. This state can no longer back down, given the international balance of power between revolution and fascism. Meanwhile, in Geneva, the International Law Commission ranks it alongside Chile, Rhodesia, Spain, India, etc. It cannot justify the emergency laws, etc. in any way other than by continuing to advance a policy that is based on the threat we pose.

So if by speculating about an amnesty you want to introduce high treason as an alternative charge to §129 at the trial,[5] this can only be reasonably suggested on the basis of the idea of one of us recanting, i.e., by fulfilling what the AGO has hoped to achieve with three-and-a-half years of isolation.

---

4   Helmut Schmidt, chancellor of West Germany from 1974 to 1982, in a statement about the occupation of the German embassy in Stockholm by the RAF's Holger Meins Commando in April 1975; see Moncourt and Smith, 339–40.

5   §129 of the criminal code, "membership in a criminal organization," later amended by §129a, "membership in a terrorist organization."

And, with this, you're putting *me* on the spot; you're making me look like someone who doesn't have her lawyer on her side, or who—let's assume—could be separated from the rest of the prisoners from the RAF even without a lawyer, or with a lawyer who is on the same page as the AGO. That's what your project signals to the AGO, even if you might not grasp that right now.

I don't feel like going on and on about this right now—besides, the smear campaigns have been going on for five years, and everybody sees them for what they are: state security's psychological warfare constructs against us, the alleged contradictions within the group, and the simple fact of their intended brainwashing project, including stereotactic intervention, targeting me specifically, because they speculated that a woman like me, much mediatized in the psychological warfare campaign, rendered an ideologized cretin, would provide propaganda for the AGO's extermination strategy against our politics. If you support this AGO project with a construct like high treason, generally speaking and also as my lawyer, you expose us/me to new measures against us. Think about it.

In 1973, the project was to kill Andreas and to cretinize me.[6] The project to kill Andreas has not been abandoned by state security nor has the project to psychiatrize all of us. Of course, if they could, they would continue the project against me: cretinization. Well, enough.

We reject it—high treason—so let it go. I would put it like this: obviously, anything a lawyer does wrong always impacts all the prisoners and the overall defense, just as it affects everyone when a lawyer does the right thing. In any case, an individual mandate relationship can only be a relationship of possession, which is bullshit. The correct conclusion is that the state forced the individual mandates upon us—we didn't want them, we wanted a group defense. For us, the fact that the state broke up the group defense also means that you have to try harder to grasp the big picture than if there were joint defense meetings between lawyers and prisoners—which is our demand.

So either you are an absent-minded professor and already completely exhausted by the university business, its performance and

---

6   In 1973, Andreas Baader was deprived of water for six days during the first hunger strike and for twelve days during the second hunger strike. Regarding Ulrike, see note 2 above.

competitive pressures, or you are pursuing a social democratic project with this mandate against us—either possibility is unacceptable. The third possibility is that it is difficult for you to learn in practice, because even if the university is not a free space, there are, of course, no base-superstructure confrontations as violent as those in the real world, only mediated conflicts—while here, as an intellectual, you are facing a machine based on the application of material force, on physical destruction, because it's not enough to psychologically destroy or physically contain the captured guerrillas. So far, I don't think you've taken this reality seriously enough. You seem to be more afraid of your material existence being disturbed than you are of being coopted by the AGO and used against us. In other words, you can't avoid making a decision for us or against us—for or against the lives of the prisoners—for or against the AGO's extermination strategy. You have to decide.

Documents from the 1975–1976 Discussion

After the third hunger strike, the prisoners' discussion turned to preparing for the trials. The discussion was not only about the way the trials were to be conducted and the political content of the evidentiary motions and the statements but, above all, about the self-understanding and relationship of each person with regard to themselves and to the others in the collective. During this period, many experiences and insights from the time underground were analyzed. Two of the texts published here relate directly to the political statements at the Stammheim trial, while the other four are reactions to letters from other prisons. They were distributed together as a "package" to all prisoners from the RAF.

To the Prisoners in Hamburg
October 7, 1975

> "The native cures himself of colonial neurosis by thrusting out the settler through force of arms."[1]

Criticism should not be chauvinist. Its role is not to put someone else down. It is a process, and it is practical—*solely* practical—which means oriented toward the goal: the struggle against the state. And *only* collectively. "That is why any individual who disregards the collective will and does not try to create it, to arouse it, to spread it, to strengthen it,

---

[1] Jean-Paul Sartre, "Preface," in Frantz Fanon, *The Wretched of the Earth* (New York: Grove Press, 1963 [1961]), 21.

to organize it, is nothing more than a fly, a 'prophet unarmed,' a fire-brand." (Gramsci)[2]

This cannot be done repressively. It must serve emancipation, or it will not be at all. That doesn't mean that it's wrong to exert pressure. The pressure that we exert does no more than convey the sharpness of the antagonism—that is, of reality, of our understanding of the situation.

Or Andreas: "Every effort at self-respect that does not recognize the antagonism, i.e., that is not based in struggle, leads to betrayal, and, as such, to self-destruction."

What is the process "unity-criticism/self-criticism-unity" *oriented* toward, if not an ongoing process, a component of the struggle against?

It *must* play a role in the struggle. So you can explain to people what they *objectively* are, how they *appear*, what they objectively do, whereas dodges like Becker's "you say one thing, but you mean another" are bullshit, the ruse of a criminalist. One means what one says. If one thinks something else, one should say so, one should struggle to be able to say it, to *find* the words, the sentences, the facts, the terms—to *search* for them.

What appears to be psychological, to be psychological crap, is rooted in the imperialist process, in class conflicts, no matter how consciously or unconsciously.

The contents are objective, but the process is subjective.

So what comes out in the process is not simply judgments but is and can only be an understanding of the objective situation as something subjective, as an expression of our relationship to it: struggle.

Yesterday, Andreas said that subjectivity, the freedom *we* mean, is certainly the most difficult thing, and there is no model for it.

You have to figure out for yourself *how* to write whatever you write by writing it, as well as determining what you are missing, what matters, what you need to do in order to accomplish what you want, to assert yourself.

In our isolation, how is it that the old stuff can assert itself, actually become dominant—even when you don't want it to?

The external cause works by means of the internal one—but what we have learned here from Andreas is that the struggle against the

---

2   Antonio Gramsci, *Philosophie der Praxis, eine Auswahl* (Frankfurt: Fischer Verlag, 1967), 362. Translation by the editors.

internal cause is waged in the struggle against the external one, the state, and in the struggle for the collective process. You *become* functional for the struggle in the struggle against—that is, through practice, which is war. And that means attacking the apparatus, organizing the collective process, finding the words *in order to understand.*

Willpower is not a possession; it is the motor. It necessarily *becomes* strong by fighting. "You have to wrest it from the machinery every day."

By contrast, the situation in the hole, letting the process drift, not addressing and solving problems, is deadly, about which Andreas says: "We once knew that only in the struggle—that is, in practical experience—is there a moment of harmony. It is human beings' 'harmonious relationship' with regards to imperialism. In it, alienation is understood and negated as a moment of *identity.*"

One reason for the depoliticization shit among some of you is that you haven't grasped the dimensions of the process over the past five years. That's why it's important to understand what it means: the state reaction conveys it.

When *La Stampa* (along with the entire foreign press) writes: "West Germany is a state that continuously violates its constitution," and West Germany is understood around the world as the center of US counterrevolution in Western Europe—that is a result of the fact that it is also understood domestically as reactionary, as a center of counterinsurgency.

The process of domestic militarization toward a police state has become visible because of us, taking on these particular contours—the *Radikalenerlass,*[3] computerized files on the entire left, recording and surveilling all its relationships and movements, as well as the emergency laws and the breaches in the exclusion of the lawyers and now our exclusion.

However, visible is not enough. The way the reactionary process is unfolding—not as they intended it, but rushed in reaction to us—it is dysfunctional. It collides with us, is made visible by the hysteria, by

---

3   *Radikalenerlass:* a decree issued in January 1972 by the Conference of Ministers of the Interior under the chairmanship of Chancellor Willy Brandt, which led to the screening of 3.5 million people in the public service by the intelligence services and more than 1,500 professional bans (*Berufsverbote*).

the violation of rights that has become the rule, by the irrationality of the method behind Prinzing's rulings, and so on.[4]

(Well, the way he rages against the experts, who, after all, are also only testifying on the basis of imperialist science, is dysfunctional, but he has no option but to carry out the struggle against us in this way, because this machine is colliding with our subjectivity.)

Armed struggle drives the entire imperialist process in its global defensive. That's what we need to understand.

So, work for it and fight for it, always, daily, continuously.

This Is How We Now See It
February 1976

This is how we now see it:

For the defense—

We don't demand to be recognized as prisoners of war. We don't demand the status, but the offensive line is resistance. The right to resistance based on international law. The defensive line is: the application, to the prisoners from the RAF and other social-revolutionary movements, of conditions of detention that correspond to the minimum guarantees of the Geneva Convention concerning the treatment of prisoners of war.

The offensive line is: resistance. It encompasses everything that can be developed as a legal argument in relation to the RAF's politics: Vietnam, the wars waged by capital in its peripheries, aggression, genocide, crimes against the civilian population, bombing of civilian infrastructure—dams, hospitals, schools—as well as defoliation and destruction of the ecosystem, etc.

Resistance draws its legitimacy from the character and function of imperialist legality—against it—or, in other words, the necessity for "illegality" results from the fascist character of imperialist legality. The connection is the result of proletarian internationalism, in the context of which we fight here on the outer lines, against the government's

---

4   Theodor Prinzing, presiding judge at the Stammheim trial. Among other things, he appointed medical experts to determine whether the defendants were fit to appear in court.

domestic and foreign policies. As such, it is important to analyze the specific structure of the German state.

Its foundation as a product of the growth of US capital during the Cold War—its economic, political, and military dependence on the US due to the total penetration of US capital; its political dependence, as demonstrated by the Yom Kippur War,[5] during which Brandt protested the transfer of arms to Israel through the port at Bremerhaven but failed to get anything done before being deposed six months later;[6] the same is true regarding the use of West German territory as a hinterland for the US military machine during its operations in Vietnam—logistics, troop rotations, supply bases, etc.

Meaning: resistance against imperialist legality, legitimized by the fascist character of the latter, is to be argued not on the basis of the offence but based on the fact of clandestine "illegality," i.e., based on the organization, as legally defined by §129 of the criminal code.[7]

This is at the root of our understanding of the organization—which does not mean that there should be a centralized leadership and coordination at all levels but an understanding of the line, the means, the moment, and the targets of the intervention: the strategy. This must be developed. This is also the argument against the AGO's claim that there exists a hierarchical gang structure in the RAF, which is being used against Andreas in particular.

This cannot be countered by merely clarifying the purpose of this psychological warfare line as a smear campaign laying the groundwork for liquidation. Plausibility and evidence—and, thus, the practical denial which alone can provide credibility—can only be achieved by talking about our structure:

Collectivity, not as a fetish but as what it really is: the autonomy of each of us.

---

5   In October 1973, Egypt and Syria attacked Israel in what is known as the Yom Kippur War. This was followed by an oil embargo that lasted for five months and led to a major restructuring of the international oil market.
6   In June 1973, Willy Brandt was the first German chancellor to visit Israel. During the so-called Yom Kippur War, the Brandt government sent weapons to Israel. The United States used the Bremerhaven port to send weapons to Israel as well. Brandt was forced to resign in 1974, after a media campaign that culminated in the discovery that his assistant Günter Guillaume was an East German spy.
7   §129 of the criminal code, "membership in a criminal organization," later amended by §129a, "membership in a terrorist organization."

The military structure, which is determined by the political line. Each individual's utmost effort and responsibility on the basis of a line that has been elaborated collectively and to which we are all committed, but which in each action and in every situation can be autonomously applied and, thus, can also be modified in practice. This means: autonomy for the groups within the framework of a consensus, of a strategy and its tactical application.

Inside the group: collectivity.

From the outside, it appears blatantly authoritarian—insofar as it aims to impose itself, its politics, its goals. Obviously, the revolution, revolutionary politics, is "the most authoritarian thing in the world," and has nothing to do with bourgeois libertinage or any romantic ideas about equality—which in this society can only be a variant of alienation. Conversely, authoritarian structures of superiority and subordination, the structure of Stalinist apparatuses, are antagonistic to guerrilla warfare, because they imply dependence and a lack of reason, of comprehension, and of transparent decision-making. Authority does not mean constraint and can never undermine communication and persuasion—the attempt to clarify the politics in order to impose them—always on the level and to the degree that are necessary and possible.

Regarding the defensive line: prison conditions for the prisoners from the RAF and other social revolutionary movements corresponding to the minimum guarantees of the Geneva Convention concerning the treatment of prisoners of war. This must be developed in relation to and against the illegal space that counterinsurgency as a means of warfare represents, the space in which the guerrilla/state confrontation plays out, and in which the prisoners from the RAF are nothing but objects in the hands of state security, which programmatically—Buback in *Der Spiegel*[8]—liquidates, eliminates, and overrides all legal norms, something that is legitimized by the legislative and legal institutions (the Supreme Court and the Constitutional Court). (Violation of the law and the constitution by the Supreme Court and the Constitutional Court, the legalization of torture; the judiciary as a mere propaganda

---

8   Attorney General Siegfried Buback expressed his views on the Stammheim trial in an interview published in *Der Spiegel* on February 15, 1976.

tool [Kitson];[9] in the case of the media, psychological warfare instead of public scrutiny and open information; integration of the repressive and ideological state apparatuses into the centralized state security apparatus, which is controlled by the BKA and the AGO.)

Fighting Together
March 1976
———————

Fighting together is also the problem with the "Umschluss" and small-group isolation[10]—which is how Amnesty defines the current measures.

Torture is a weapon in the war that the counterinsurgency machine—made up of the BKA, the Attorney General's Office, the judiciary, the prison system, and the government—is waging against us. Psychiatric torture is the approach adopted by social democracy. The science of counterinsurgency is the method adopted by imperialism on the defensive. The system's loss of legitimacy obliges it to make use of subterfuge and manipulation.

With regard to public opinion, their plan was to destroy us secretly in order to then put us on display—cretinized—so that the people (who

———————

9   British Army General Frank Kitson was one of the foremost experts on "low-intensity" counterinsurgency warfare. His book, based on his experiences in Kenya, Malaysia, Oman, Cyprus, and Northern Ireland, has long been used as a manual for NATO special forces; Frank Kitson, *Low Intensity Operations* (London: Faber & Faber, 1991 [1971]).

10 "Umschluss" is a term used by the prison administration to signify a situation in which two or three prisoners are allowed to see each other for a few hours in a cell. Isolation in small groups in high-security wards, denounced by Amnesty International and addressed later in this letter, does not allow for effective social interaction. During the Stammheim trial, medical experts appointed by the court were of the opinion that effective interaction was only possible in groups of at least ten to fifteen people, which never happened. From the first day of their incarceration, the political prisoners were isolated from everyone else in order to break down their collective identity and encourage them to repent. Most were held in cells surrounded by empty cells, in completely unoccupied wings, or in high security wings. Their contacts were limited, mainly to family members and lawyers (see "Interview During the Hunger Strike," this volume, pp. 44–47). Following each clandestine action on the outside, they were deprived of their radios, newspapers, and all contact. Later, these conditions were relaxed, allowing them to meet or to associate in two- to four-person groups in the high-security wings. During the Stammheim trial, in the two years before her death, Ulrike was able to spend time with Gudrun Ensslin, Andreas Baader, and Jan Raspe.

don't know what happened in between: the torture) will think that is what we are: cretins.

The problem is that if we ourselves don't understand what is being done to us, it works. That's how it was in the tower[11]—the counterinsurgency methods were tested in West Berlin and then perfected in West Germany.

That's how it was for Gudrun and me.[12]

You cannot treat the other person as the determining factor in your suffering in this situation. It is the machine, and you can only confuse it with the other person if you have made him or her your object or if you have been reduced to an object yourself, something that can only happen when you get to the point that you no longer fight. No longer fight to remain conscious: of yourself, of the others, of the situation, and of everything that is happening, whatever information, people, or events present themselves.

That means that in the situation of being totally legalized, subject to absolute control by the state and complete coercion, you naturally behave in a clandestine way, otherwise you will become what they want you to be: a cretin—a former combatant and, thus, someone who is once again legal.

By "in a clandestine way," I mean: twenty-four-hour-a-day self-determination; and that is how you come together with the others—because there is *nothing* you can take for granted in the "Umschluss" or small-group isolation without the risk of exploiting the other person.

That is entirely logical.

Because even when we were still legal we understood that one cannot live under imperialism without waging war against it—how could that be different in the enforced legality of prison?—otherwise one only understood a small part of all that shit. But now, in prison and faced with torture, one understands the *entire* thing, the war. One fights to understand and one understands to fight, or else one is broken.

The struggle to understand is not about being right —never—but about doing what you do, what you want to do, what you have to do, the

---

11 The "tower" was a high-security section in the Moabit men's prison in West Berlin, where the female prisoners were held on a number of occasions, including during their trials.

12 Gudrun Ensslin and Ulrike Meinhof were both in the silent wing at Ossendorf prison in Cologne for three months.

right way; that is, creating movement and not confusion or stagnation or ownership or domination.

The goal is the struggle, the struggle that engenders struggle—which is something that never works against the other person. It *only* works if we are together. And coming together is more than the negation of the shitty "repressive dual relationship." Coming together is the abolition of competition and of all the pressure and demands that come with it. Coming together—as I see it—is the embryonic form of communism, of direct exchange between producers, in which the negation of money occurs. It is eliminated and new forms of exchange arise—but they can only be developed in the struggle, in the *war* against imperialism.

And there is no question that torture is part of this war, and so isolation is also an opportunity—because it is part of the war, and because, faced with it, we are not isolated from our raison d'être: the war.

Thus, as part of the war, the struggle in prison has its own relevance. To deny this, as the 2nd of June Movement does, constitutes military fetishism and a failure to grasp the totality of this war: that to act is political—that to struggle is political.

To Hanna[13]
March 19, 1976

The politicians' drivel is not what the people think but what the politicians want them to think. And when they say "we," they try to blather in such a way that people recognize their own thoughts and way of thinking in it and take it as being well said. But the state wouldn't need opinion polls, nor would it need its intelligence services, if indoctrination by psychological warfare was as simple as that.

As Gramsci said, the legal country is not the real country; or more plainly stated: the dominant opinion is not the opinion of the dominated. What you say is bullshit. You reason in the realm of the imaginary, as if the enemy is the ideology which he sputters, the drivel, the platitudes that they've drummed into you from their bag of tricks with the politicians' cadence of consensus, as if the media and the people whom

13 Hanna Krabbe, a member of the RAF's Holger Meins Commando, was in prison from 1975 to 1996.

they pour all this shit on were one and the same thing. It is not real, it is the product of the counterinsurgency machine consisting of the BKA, the AGO, the government, the media, the intelligence services, etc.

As if the enemy were not material but spiritual.

You don't ask yourself what the condition that Brandt[14] calls "normal" really is—and you don't recognize in Buback's statement that he has determined the conflict—war in all its dimensions—to be international, and that he speaks as a representative of US capital's international interests. You find it "absurd," and instead of analyzing it, you offer a *word*—"CIA"—which is a metaphor for Buback's morally decadent policy—and which is gratuitous. You thereby incriminate yourself, because, in practice, you whine about the fact that this is war, *after* having clearly stood on our side in this war and having begun to fight.

Your text could be addressed to the US civil rights movement, which begs the question: If that is how you see things, why are you not there but here with us?

In any event, you are here.

The internationalism that you have fought for and for which you became part of the RAF is not that of international, inter-state organizations like the United Nations and Geneva; it is the internationalism of the war against imperialism being waged by the liberation movements in the Third World and in the capitalist centers.

War—that's what it is. You won't find your bearings here by relying on rumors, but *only* by studying the facts and their connection to the class struggle.

If in isolation you do not make the effort to persistently and continuously analyze *reality* by defining it and its material content in the context of the struggle—class struggle understood as war—then you will become "blank," out of touch, sick, which means you will develop a sick relationship with regard to reality. That is betrayal by capitulation in the face of the reality of torture and the effort demanded by resistance, which otherwise is just a word.

It is not acceptable—in isolation, you can't permit yourself, on top of everything else, to torment yourself. That, as Andreas has said, doesn't mean that you can avoid suffering certain experiences in the process

---

14   Willy Brandt, former SPD chancellor of West Germany.

of liberation from alienation. But it is one thing to slave away in order to understand the politics, the facts, the context, and the group so as to act; it is another to just slave away because isolation strips you of all illusions about yourself, which can be a very bitter pill to swallow.

And if it is the case that your capacity to act is based on socialization through fear and despair, then that's the starting point from which you fight.

Eventually you might perhaps understand—I don't know—that one can only achieve something with words if they contain the understanding of the real situation, the one in which everyone finds themself under imperialism: that wanting to agitate with words makes no sense, because *only* clarity agitates, only truth.

Given the environment in which we are fighting—the post-fascist state, consumer culture, metropolitan chauvinism, mass media manipulation, psychological warfare, social democracy—and faced with the repression that confronts us here, indignation is not a weapon. It is pointless and empty. Whoever is truly indignant, that is to say, is concerned and engaged, does not scream but reflects on what can be done.

That's the SPK[15]—replacing the struggle with screams. It is not simply distasteful, it destroys you in isolation, because it means opposing brutal, material repression with nothing more than ideology, instead of with mental effort, which is also physical.

Arm the masses—that is still what capital is doing: the cops, the army, the far right. So before you glorify the West German masses, or "the masses" in general, think about what it's really like here. Ho wrote in *L'Humanité*,[16] in 1922, "The masses are fundamentally ready for rebellion but completely ignorant. They want to liberate themselves, but they don't know how to begin."

That is not our situation.

What we are concentrating on most right now is how we can convey in a way that can be understood, even if you're not in a similar situation, the at times gruesome experiences we have had in isolation,

---

15   SPK, the Socialist Patients Collective, whose motto was: turn illness into a weapon. Several individuals who had been active in the SPK would later join the RAF.

16   Vietnam's president Ho Chi Minh was a founder and the chairman of the Vietnamese Communist Party from 1941 until his death in 1969, at the age of seventy-nine. In 1922 he was living in Paris and was involved in the anticolonial and communist movements there. *L'Humanité* is the newspaper of the French Communist Party.

for which the terms are betrayal, capitulation, self-destruction, depoliti-cization. For if it is true that in the guerrilla each one can learn from the others, then it must be possible to convey our experiences—the condi-tion for which is understanding collectivity as a process—a process for which the institutionalization of presumed authorities is antagonistic.

Understanding collectivity as a process means fighting *together*— against the machine, which is real and not imaginary.

Class Position
April 13, 1976

We are beginning to find it generally unbearable—the class position with which you puff yourself up there. It's also not a question of defi-nition, because the *struggle* has been omitted in it, i.e., the essential.

It doesn't exist. It is a pedestal that has very little in common with what *we* want. What we want is the revolution. That means, there is the goal, and, with regard to the goal, there isn't a position but *only* move-ment, the struggle. To *be* the relationship, as you say, means: to fight.

There is the situation of the class: proletariat, proletarianization, declassing, humiliation, abuse, expropriation, servitude, poverty.

Under imperialism, the complete penetration of all relationships by the market and the penetration of society by repressive and ideo-logical state structures leave no place and no time where you can say: this is my starting point. There is only illegality, the underground and liberated territories, i.e., the underground as an offensive position for revolutionary intervention, which you will also not find just like that but which is itself a moment of attack, i.e., without it it is nonexistent.

The class position corresponds to Soviet foreign policy presented as the class position of the international proletariat, and the USSR's accumulation model presented as socialism.

It is the position of—the apology for— "socialism in one coun-try," and that means that it is an ideology of domination, that was determined not offensively out of its contradiction to imperialism but defensively out of the constraints of encirclement.

You can say that Soviet domestic and foreign policy was histori-cally necessary, but you can't adopt what it declared to be absolute as a class position. The class position—that is to say, the interest, the need, the mission of the class to struggle for communism so as to be able to live—is left implicit in this policy. I would say it is cancelled out by it, which is absurd. Position and movement are mutually exclusive. It is a construct geared at justification—an assertion.

It asserts that the politics of the class are derived from the economy, which is incorrect. The politics of the class are the result of its confrontation with the politics of capital, and the politics of capital are a function of its economy. Where I think Poulantzas is right is where he says that the economic activities of the state are part of its repressive and ideological functions[17]—class struggle.

The politics of the class are its struggle against the politics of capital and not against the economy, which, directly or by way of the state, proletarianizes the class. The class position of the proletariat is war—that is a contradiction in itself—nonsense. The Soviet Union talks about the class position because it wants to present its state policy as part of the class struggle. What I am saying is that it is the expression of Soviet foreign policy. Which means, they can be allies in the process of liberation, but not protagonists. Protagonists have no position—they have a goal.

The "class position" has always been a cudgel. It is always the claim to possess and bestow, by way of the party apparatus, a conception of reality different from reality as it is perceived and experienced. Specifically, it is a claim to a position of struggle without class struggle. As you say, it is "from this position" that we still have to act, rather than acting already.

In 1969, it was the ML, KSV, and AO who, with the "class position," depoliticized the movement in the universities by supporting policies that no student could relate to emotionally.[18] It was a liquidationist position against the anti-imperialist protest movement, and I think that is the horror of this term and of what it represents, the fact that it rules out the possibility of emotional identification with proletarian politics—it is a catechism.

We are *not* starting from a class position, but from class *struggle* as the principle of all history, and from class *war* as the reality within

---

17   Nicos Poulantzas, *Political Power and Social Classes* (London: New Left Books, 1978).
18   The KPD/ML, the KSV, and the KPD/AO were self-styled Marxist-Leninist groups active in West Germany at the time.

which proletarian politics are realized—and, as we have seen, *only* in and by war.

The class position can only be the *movement* of the class in the class war, the world proletariat engaged in armed struggle, its true vanguards, the liberation movements.

Or, as George Jackson[19] said, "connections, connections, connections." So, movement, interaction, communication, coordination, fighting together—strategy.

All of this is paralyzed in the term "class position"—and that is also how you use it when you try to convince Inga.[20] But you should know by now that there is hardly anything more repulsive than being fed complete nonsense.

In other words, the class position is a triumphalist position.

Certainly, there is also something heroic about it. However, that's not what we want. What we want is to have an effect.

But enough. I have the impression that I'm talking to a wall, and that is not the point of all of this. The goal is to have you climb down from your pedestal.

So, come on down. You're boasting.

Fragment Regarding the Structure of the Group
April 1976

Collectivity is a key element in the guerrilla's structure, and—subjectivity being assumed to be the precondition of each person's decision to fight—its most important one. The collective is a group that thinks, feels, and acts as a group.

Leadership in the guerrilla consists of the individual or individuals who keep the collective process of the group open and organize it in the process of its practice: anti-imperialist struggle, based on each individual's self-determination and decision to be an element of the intervention, understanding that what he or she wants to achieve can only be achieved collectively, and it means the group in which

19 Cf. George Jackson, *Soledad Brother: The Prison Letters of George Jackson* (Chicago: Lawrence Hill Books, 1970).

20 Inga Hochstein, a political prisoner in Hamburg sentenced to ten years in prison.

everything it is—military, policy, strategy, embryonic form of the new society—is practically and concretely contained in its process as a group that is committed to anti-imperialist struggle

The line, based on the strategy, the logic, and the rationality of the individual tactical steps (actions)—is developed collectively. It is the result of a process of discussion informed by everyone's experiences and knowledge, and is, therefore, collectively formulated and, thus, becomes binding. In other words, the line is developed from the process of the practice and the analysis of its conditions, experience, and anticipation. Which is possible as a unified process because there is unanimity regarding the goal and the willpower to achieve it.

Once the line has been developed and understood, the group's practice can be coordinated according to a military command structure. Its execution requires absolute discipline, and, at the same time, absolute autonomy, that is to say, an autonomous orientation and decision-making capacity regardless of the circumstances.

What unites the guerrilla at all times is each individual's determination to carry on the struggle. [...]

Once again, we must not forget that all revolutionary initiatives that have provided direction, coherence, continuity, and, thus, political power to an objectively natural process—we think here of the mass strike wave in Russia in 1905 and the October Revolution—encouraged individuals to develop their resolve and willpower and were initiated by the resolve and willpower of individuals.

For Gramsci, willpower is the essential precondition; strong willpower as the engine of the revolutionary process, in which subjectivity becomes practical.

Statements and Preparations for the Trials

In January 1976, at the Stammheim trial, Andreas, Gudrun, Ulrike, and Jan delivered a comprehensive statement about their politics. They also intervened several times during the defense motions in court. The texts presented here are part of the discussions and the documents written in preparation for the trials against RAF members, as well as the reconstruction of statements made at the Stammheim trial.

Extracts from the Stammheim Trial Statement January 1976

We're really not into proclamations, and certainly a proclamation would be pointless given the nature of the pseudo-public attending these proceedings—the distorted, corrupted, and totally manipulated public who (as Wunder puts it)[1] is permitted to observe.

The problem is—and this is also part of these pathetic proceedings and why they're happening in this building in Stammheim and not in a city where the legal left can mobilize—pretty much nobody here is listening to what we say for any reason other than cheap sensationalism, or else with the ear of an informant or of the market. This market cannot absorb the content and in the case of our political destruction not even the facts. If the public, which is permitted entry and allowed to observe, were to serve a public control function, this trial would be impossible.

---

[1] Heinrich Wunder, one of the federal prosecutors.

This project, in the verbiage of the politicians, in the very military character of the trial, in the corrupt worm sitting up front, in the imperial self-promotion that determines every detail of these pathetic proceedings, is pure demagogy, based on five years of rabble-rousing psychological warfare.

We are fighting on a terrain that has been meticulously arranged, and I don't intend to elaborate on that any further at this point. Everyone knows by now that all illegal means have been and are being explored and used to render us incapable of defending ourselves, which is in keeping with the nature of a militarized judiciary—a judiciary incapable of political articulation in this confrontation, a reality the state must fear, because that is at the core of the entire exercise. It conveys the revolutionary character of the confrontation as much as it determines the state's attempt to cope, this whole enormous attempt to stir up a reactionary mobilization, including its expression here in the architecture—as counterrevolution, as class war.

That's why we're here. We're participating in this trial, or at least have tried to, to expose and interpret its pitiful nature and the fact that the state is forced to use any and all means—Schmidt[2] has said so often enough—to wrest legitimacy from four prisoners—while in the process exposing its weakness.

The argument that we should provide a scientific explanation of our politics (which I think we are able to do now) would, however, be absurd in this context. Our only interest is to develop a concept—based on our experience and analysis—the legal publication of which the AGO cannot prevent if it is presented here. We have decided *against* a detailed presentation of the concept of revolutionary strategy here at this point in time for three reasons:

Ulrike:

In any case, Prinzing[3] would interrupt us, because it would take too long, and because he understands that his job here as a state security judge is to keep political content out of these proceedings.

Second, the text will be analyzed—this is our experience, and we are not certain that by reconstructing the strategic reasoning we would

---

2   Helmut Schmidt, West German chancellor.
3   Theodor Prinzing, presiding judge at the Stammheim trial.

not be providing state security with weapons, without also being able to make them available for the organization of revolutionary politics.

Finally—and this is also important—we speak only for the prisoners on the basis of their discussions and for ourselves. We do not speak for the groups that are fighting underground.

All that to say: the continuity of the urban guerrilla, the continuity of its revolutionary attack, is conveyed by its actions and in no particular way by the statements of its imprisoned members.

A detailed presentation of the *context*—such a pretention would in itself be an error, because all these proceedings are irrelevant to the development of the urban guerrilla.

We also think that an attempt at a scientific explanation presupposes a minimal consensus, that of disputation. That would be a contradiction in itself in a venue where it is so openly and brutally absent, if only given the miserable measures Prinzing has taken to prevent this text from being presented. Never mind the fact that this court has proven for months that it is unable and unwilling to follow any argument of substance.

The scientific concept of our politics—the theoretical justification on the basis of the 1970 analysis alone would be totally meaningless to this court. It would only be useful for state security analysts, given that five years of urban guerrilla activity have proven its accuracy.

Making a statement also always means defending something against the brutal machinations going on here, which means engaging with the process, as if we were confessing. It would be an interaction that would oblige us to engage with this court, with this entire process. That is simply impossible—tactically as well—and it has become even more impossible over the course of the last three years. The content of these proceedings is of no concern to us. We are only concerned with the measures and the chance to explain them. Andreas has already said a lot about that, and we will probably say some more during the evidentiary motions—we'll have to see.

Now, Andreas or we will briefly, at least relatively briefly, be pursuing the lines of discussion—since Zeis[4] snatched our written documents and an at least theoretically important manuscript right before the trial—to talk about two aspects of the issue:

---

4   Peter Zeis, one of the federal prosecutors.

1. The *necessity* of our politics based on a historical determination and the concrete process of resistance from which the RAF emerged five years ago; and on that basis:
2. The *possibility* of planning the revolutionary process that anticipates the urban guerrilla as a tactic, as a fragment of a fragment.

Given the level of abstraction that the trial has now reached through Prinzing's narrow-minded, worm-like, and brutal adherence to established criminal procedure, we really have no choice but to respond with our own abstractions. It should be made clear at this point that this was not our intention at the outset. It was not our plan to confront this trial with the contents of revolutionary politics, presenting them here as if it were a seminar. We planned to give one or more short explanations and imagined making it more concrete during the defense motions.

That's it for our understanding of the setting. In the meantime, it has become clear that we probably can't do that, because we are in very poor shape, which was probably Prinzing's plan, as he has fought with all the means at his disposal to undermine our ability to defend ourselves, and with what he calls the "final" regulation of our prison conditions, with which our partial inability to appear is to be solidified and then further intensified. And what's more, because he would also directly prevent it by quashing motions for the admission of evidence, just as he has quashed *every* defense motion for the past six months. This simply means that the reality and context of our politics cannot be presented during evidentiary hearings. So we will try to explain this by attempting the ritual of a basic statement, which is, however, fragmentary, at least as far as our analysis goes. Quite a bit of what would be important in this regard, the AGO seized just before the trial.

Andreas:

At this point, things are determined by the absurd conditions and are actually dependent upon us not being interrupted. If Prinzing continues to interrupt us, we will stop, because we have only a partial manuscript and have not been able to discuss it in much detail. We can always publish it later, when it is more clearly structured.

The whole attempt to make this available through the court records is, to be more precise, determined by the international discussion of the militant anti-revisionist left in Europe, and not only in Europe. We want to show how the encirclement and complete integration of the traditional proletarian class organizations into the politics of capital in West Germany is historically conditioned, and we are attempting to show how this process can only be smashed internationally, through the international political reconstruction of the proletariat, with a class strategy based on how capitalist conditions are developing. The guerrilla in the capitalist centers is the conscious expression, the interpretation, the conscious subjective attempt to mediate this reconstruction within and on the basis of its international dimension.

To describe this, to make it clear, we *must* also address economic categories. It can only be developed, no matter how fragmentarily and how truncated, based on the concept of objective tendency (this tendency not being at the conceptual level of Schmidt but of Marx—*Grundrisse*).[5]

Certainly, this is unusual, and I have never heard of such a thing being attempted at a political trial, but it is not just a reaction to the attempt, the tedious demagogic attempt, to ensure that this trial be devoid of any political *content*. The crime, as Sartre said, lies in wanting to treat us like criminals—although we, of course, are okay with that, insofar as revolutionary politics, and not only revolutionary politics but any attempt at democratic social opposition in this state, will necessarily be criminalized and is being criminalized. Nor do we have any problem with the form of resistance that class justice refers to as common criminality.

It is, in fact, a *practical* attempt to break through the censorship and the criminalization of our texts; what we say here can be published, as things are at this point. Although Buback will surely come up with some brutal way to sabotage that, we will try nonetheless. (That's precisely why we will make no concessions to those who are listening here.)

A fact, which I will briefly repeat once again, is that we (and by this I mean the prisoners) are all certain that developments confirm our analysis and our practice, just as has been the case for five years.

We made mistakes, but we would say that they were objectively necessary mistakes due to the weakness of proletarian politics in West Germany.

---

5   Karl Marx, *Grundrisse: Foundations of the Critique of Political Economy* (London: Penguin Classics, 1993 [1857–1861]).

And—lest this text encourage the opposite view—in the RAF, there is no separation between theoreticians and practitioners—the sort of division of labor, exploitation, and hierarchical structure that psychological warfare projects onto us. There was perfect clarity among all of us about how to conceptualize and determine the difficulties, problems, and structure of an underground combatant group. Our assessment of the need for such a group has not changed. However, we have learned that the underground is also the only liberated territory in the class war where human relations are possible. We have also become subjectively acquainted with its emancipatory, its liberating, dialectic. We have nothing—or little—to say here about learning processes, existential radicalism, and collective structures, because, in the meantime, the reaction of the imperialist SPD state—the counterpropaganda and the brutal state security repression against us, which must clearly be understood as counterinsurgency—has also become propaganda *for* us. It conveys the dimensions and relevance of proletarian politics and of the attack by small armed underground groups that determine the strategy necessary to oppose capital and the imperialist state in the international context of anti-imperialist liberation struggles during this phase of imperialism's strategic defensive.

Ulrike:

The group's leadership structure is worth mentioning here, because psychological warfare uses personalization as a way to divide the proletariat. It individualizes revolutionary politics to prevent them from being understood as the politics of the class, while at the same time preparing the propaganda terrain for the physical liquidation of individual combatants.

Isolation was meant to break up the group, and the AGO's plan was to cretinize me, first using the silent wing, then with an attempted stereotactic intervention; at the same time, in the summer of 1973, during our hunger strike, Andreas was to be murdered by water deprivation. We have proven this to be a fact; there is nothing speculative about it. Holger was murdered *because* he had a leadership role in the group; that is, he was an element of orientation in the group.

The guerrilla is a cadre organization—the goal of its collective learning process is the equality of the fighters, the implication of each individual in the collective, their analytical and practical empowerment and their self-reliance and ability to themselves build an armed nucleus and keep the collective learning process open. This process was initiated by Andreas in the RAF, and from the beginning of the RAF Andreas was what every combatant hopes to and must become: the embodiment of the group's politics and strategy.

The individual is the group.

Its collective process being subject to the mechanics of the hierarchical imperialist structure and the objective necessity of revolt as the expression of the individual will, are what Wunder is blathering on about when he talks about "political motivation."

(It is beyond outrageous that the representative of an authority here that directly represents the interests of US capital and the US military, which has 125 military bases and 7,000 nuclear warheads on West German territory, imagines that he can still capitalize on armed struggle against US capital and the imperialist state.)

Leadership in the guerrilla serves the function of conveying the relationship between subjectivity and necessity, willpower and objectivity, in the practice of the group, its structure, and its activity. It arises from the group process, from the complex pressures of the underground struggle that mediate the collective learning and working processes and the initiative of each individual in the collective process as an initiative based on and for further practice. Its specific role is to facilitate the continuity of the learning process, of the experience, of the interaction, and of the ability of the organization to respond to all external and internal challenges. Leadership and collectivity are not contradictory within the guerrilla. They are based on the goal being determined by each individual and, thus, by the collective and its leadership—freedom, liberation, and the experience of each individual that life and subjectivity are only possible in armed anti-imperialist struggle; armed struggle from the underground is the only possibility under imperialism for practical critical activity.

Leadership is not a function that gives rise to the group but one that arises in the process of the group's formation. It emerges from the group's practice and, thus, from its collective process, and it remains the responsibility of the individual to whom it is attributed because of his or her ability to anticipate developments and his or her commitment to keep the collective process open. Furthermore, in our experience, it is always the individual or individuals who do not desire a position of leadership, which under imperialism can only be a desire to dominate others.

In brief, we would say that leadership in the guerrilla is a matter of initiative, interaction, and always, at every moment, the assertion of the primacy of practice, of politics as proletarian politics; that is, action that resists the tendency to reproduce imperialist structures, including domination, rationalization, the division of labor, competition, and the irrational reflexes based on isolation and fear.

Andreas plays this role in the RAF, because, within the RAF, he conveys proletarian politics, i.e., insurrection, in a way meant to make leadership superfluous through collective practice, in the conceptual context of the particular within the general, of the possible within the necessary, of the subjective within the objective, and of theory *serving* practice. That's why the AGO, this court, the BKA, and the government hate Andreas the most. For them, it's about destroying the new, the new human being, the new society, whose embryonic form is the guerrilla in its expression of power, subjectivity, a learning process, and practice.

Psychological warfare must personalize, because it cannot attack what the guerrilla is actually about—the collective underground struggle against the state—without propagating the politics of the guerrilla, its freedom, which is its freedom to struggle. It must personalize in order to present the central moment of its freedom, the underground— that is, its capacity to act—as unfreedom.

However, when Herold[6] says "Baaders and Meinhofs," this plural indicates that what was meant to be conveyed by the method of personalization—namely, to make the guerrilla's actions appear to be the work of individuals—has not been conveyed. Herold, of course, cannot understand what a collective is. His plural reflects the fact that we are many, and that we fight on the basis of objective necessity, which is material. Leadership also means conveying the dialectic of possibility and necessity, and that with necessity comes the possibility of struggle— that is, the possibility to organize, to carry out attacks, and to increase their impact.

Thus, subjectively, leadership also has the function of encouragement and is a moment of mobilization. Its role rules out its institutionalization; it is as dependent on the group's collective

---

6   Horst Herold, president of the BKA, Germany's federal investigation bureau.

interaction as the group is dependent on it. It radically excludes all the dead and absolutely deadly structures of the imperialist bureaucracies. On the basis of the simple dialectic that just as the military represents the epitome of the imperialist structure, which is alienation, in the guerrilla, a military organization for proletarian politics, alienation is necessarily completely abolished. It is eliminated by the politics—or will be in the ongoing process. The guerrilla's politics form the basis of its capacity to act—they represent its potential.

We would say that the counterpropaganda that personalizes Andreas, based on concepts from the imperialist structure, has run aground. What the extent of the agitation conveys is the power of subjectivity, the power of proletarian politics—and we know that his name has long stood for rebellion. That, for many people, the state security propaganda against us has made his name the expression of what Andreas is for us: the expression—as Mao says—of "politics in command," meaning proletarian politics, the politics of the dispossessed.

The rationale behind the assertion that the RAF was political when it began but then became depoliticized indicates that state security could not find a fault line within the RAF, that Andreas provided the RAF with a revolutionary political concept from the beginning—of which the second thesis on Feuerbach says: "The question whether objective truth can be attributed to human thinking is not a question of theory but is a *practical* question. Man must prove the truth, i.e. the reality and power, the this-worldliness of his thinking in practice. The dispute over the reality or non-reality of thinking which is isolated from practice is a purely *scholastic* question."[7]

Andreas is targeted as the epitome of our politics, because he embodies the unity of analysis, collectivity, and action.

Revolutionary theory is critical theory. When we have formulated it for publication, we have defined it as a *weapon* and always related it to clearly outlined problems related to the practice of the underground struggle. Theory that has no relation to practice—that does not explain our situation and show us a way to change it—has never interested us. That is the kind of theory that psychological warfare is referring to

---

7   Karl Marx, "Theses on Feuerbach," in *Marx & Engels Collected Works*, vol. 5 (London: Lawrence & Wishart, 1975), 3.

when it elevates Mahler and me as RAF theoreticians—nothing more than newspaper columns or the alienated instrumentalization of the Marxist conceptual framework as it is dogmatically understood by the MLs—for the sake of being right, like Mahler when he wrote *Regarding the Armed Struggle in Western Europe*. The RAF's theoretical writings were meant to convince people that it is right to support the urban guerrilla and why. We treated them as weapons, because anything that benefits the underground armed struggle is a weapon.

To speak of Andreas is to speak of us, because when we say that the role of leadership is to make itself superfluous in practice, through collectivity, that means that the guerrilla, as an underground organization, is and must be a politico-military organization, and that means that everyone must become a leader, must develop the capacity to be a leader. The comprehensive formulation would be: must be empowered to learn—to go beyond experience, one's own and that of the group, as well as that of the liberation movements in the Third World, including the capacity to *communicate* their experience. Learning is only possible in the struggle against the state, against its defamatory methods, its lies and filth, against the structures of imperialist socialization and indoctrination, and this is *only* possible collectively and with the goal of succeeding through armed action.

Drawing upon Gramsci, collective leadership means that the project must be understood by everyone in the guerrilla, so that everyone recognizes his or her role in its execution and realization as part of the whole and recognizes that in undertaking a project, in initiating an action, positive and negative consequences, approval and rejection, are anticipated, and the initiative contains within itself the answers, thereby opening up terrain for the organization. That is the relationship of theory and practice.

Andreas:

The personalization of revolutionary politics in psychological warfare aims at—and is, thus, the propagandistic counterpart to—torture through isolation meant to desocialize the combatants and to depersonalize revolutionary action—action which is always understood by the masses, no matter how it is conveyed—by means of the depersonalization of the combatants, who are made to look like foreign bodies within society.

Personalization aims at making the revolutionary state of emergency appear to be everyday life in a brutal imperialist society, in order to redirect toward the guerrilla the latent hatred of the masses for the state, for state parasitism, for the repressive and ideological state apparatuses consisting of the Attorney General's Office, the judiciary, the police, etc., for the parasitic machine that does nothing but devour the surplus. The goal is to deter the people from transforming the state of emergency in which they live into a real state of emergency, a state of emergency that serves their needs. However, precisely because the machine can do nothing but project and is only able to see its own reflection, can produce nothing but can only reproduce itself, its contents, the shit it produces with its psychological warfare inevitably lands on its own feet.

In short: leadership must be the concrete conceptualization of the situation and how to transcend it: the objectives and how to communicate them *within the structure* of the combatant group/organization. Simply stated, in the necessity (that is, the history that produces the concept and, thus, the history of the group and the understanding of each individual in it: revolutionary struggle)—in the necessity of the antagonism in which we situate ourselves and our politics, that is to say, in the struggle, in the context of the *violence* and the complex pressures it imposes on the individual, freedom—liberation—is possible.

Ulrike:

Wunder's stupid idea that Andreas never worked in a factory is part of this context—psychological warfare—because it shows how, in psychological warfare, pseudo-scientific anticommunism usurps and ossifies history, prejudice, and the existing structures. His assertion is incorrect. Andreas learned and developed his understanding in the factory, on the street, and in prison. This assertion corresponds to the distortion of facts in psychological warfare and to the idea that the RAF is a group of guys and girls from the upper middle class with bourgeois socialization. If we were to base ourselves on sociology, it could be said that half of us come from proletarian backgrounds—elementary school, apprenticeships, the factory, asylums, prison. The assertion also negates—certainly also on the basis of ignorance—that with the third real subsumption at the beginning of the 1960s a process of mass proletarianization and declassing took place.

The process of massification and technocratization of the universities, media concentration, etc. was the domestic reason for the mobilization at the universities from 1966 onward. The external reason was the US war in Vietnam. Psychological warfare attempts to obscure the fact that all the militants in the RAF worked and learned in the New Left grassroots projects following Easter 1968.[8]

The struggle itself proletarianizes the fighters. "An absence of property" is the Korean party's term for the proletarian relationship to the struggle for communism: *juche* defines the proletariat as the antagonist of imperialism—that is, as the subject of liberation.[9] This is certainly not a sociological concept of the proletariat, which we would not be interested in anyway. "Proletariat" is not a concept from fascist genealogy studies—it designates a relationship. The relationship of the guerrilla to the people reflects the *relationship* of the proletariat to the imperialist state, defined as a deadly enemy, as the antagonist in the context of class war. "Proletariat" is a concept based in struggle.

Sartre says: "It is true that the proletariat carries within itself the death of the bourgeoisie; it is equally true that the capitalist system is mined by structural contradictions. But this does not necessarily imply the existence of class consciousness or of class struggle. In order that there should be consciousness and struggle, it is necessary that somebody should be fighting."[10]

So what is behind Wunder's statement? Does Wunder mean "Arbeit macht frei,"[11] i.e., the concentration camp? Is he referring to the Protestant work ethic? For example, the quote: "Labor is the source of all wealth, and of all civilization."[12] Faced with mass unemployment in 1930, there was nothing the old social democracy could do with this

---

8 The "Easter riots" in 1968 were a widespread reaction to the attempted assassination of student spokesperson Rudi Dutschke by a right-winger inspired by the Springer press.

9 "Juche" is a concept developed by North Korean President Kim Il-sung to designate the unity of the anti-imperialist struggle and the struggle for communism.

10 Jean-Paul Sartre, "Mass, Spontaneity, Party; a Conversation with Il Manifesto," in *The Social Register*, vol. 7 (August 27, 1969) (London/New York: Merlin Press/Monthly Review Press, 1970), 237.

11 "Arbeit macht frei" (work will make you free) is the inscription at the entrance to the Auschwitz concentration camp.

12 Quote from the social democratic *Gotha Program*, criticized in Karl Marx, "The Gotha and Erfurt Programs," in *Marx and Engels Collected Works*, vol. 24 (London: Lawrence & Wishart, 1975), 81.

position from the Gotha Program, given that political power had long since slipped from its hands (because the party had never managed to take control of the Ministry of War) and was finally ceded to the fascists. Marx said briefly and dryly about the mystified concept of work in the Gotha Program: "the man who possesses no other property than his labor power must, in all conditions of society and culture, be the slave of other men who have made themselves the owners of the material conditions of labor."[13]

Given this economic necessity, Marx concluded that workers had the political right to leave the factory, arm themselves, and fight the state. The only reason that we refer to Marx here is because he explained scientifically the need for insurrection, for class struggle as class *war* against the parasitic network of repressive and ideological apparatuses, against the bourgeois state.

The prosecution's drivel is pure cynicism—while there is more than 4 percent unemployment in Germany—more than one million people, and almost five million in Western Europe—the social democratic response is its own fascist "internal security" project, the integration of the repressive state apparatus in Western Europe under the command of the BKA's information monopoly, as well as the integration of the internal and external security structures within the framework of NATO, under the command of the Pentagon. (Some other time, we will say something about the political function of social democracy for US capital, its fascist project, and the institutional strategy of modern fascism.)

Just as "the legal country is not the real country" (Gramsci), the real life of the workers is not in the factory. The AGO naturally looks fondly upon the slavery of the proletariat in the factories, and Wunder, as a face of the parasitic state security machine, very logically fetishizes factory work, because if the workers stopped going to the factory—to the factory that is being referred to *here*: where work is under the command of capital—the whole clique of state security puppets who stand before us would have nothing to eat. (Wunder, as an old social democrat, as an old social democratic rat, obviously knows that in undermining and finally dismantling the repressive and ideological state apparatuses, the endpoint of our struggle is the liberation of labor.) Therefore, the

13 Ibid.

material content of the prosecution's offensive is simply this: Andreas must—we all must—feed the federal prosecutors. An acceptable human being, as the AGO sees it, is a human being who feeds the federal prosecutors—a submissive subject, a human being who exists for the state and for no other reason than for the state. As Andreas has said: "For the federal prosecution, the ideal citizen is the prisoner who keeps a photo of Buback in his closet."

A Letter from Ulrike for the Discussion in Stammheim
Early 1976

Taylorism emerged after the workers' revolts in all the emerging imperialist states—i.e., the rapid socialization of monopoly production—and was first introduced by Ford in Detroit *before* World War I. It was simultaneously both a way to reduce costs through mass production and a way to discipline the working class with higher wages. It also served to create an attachment to the company during a period in which competition was being eliminated by the formation of monopolies, as well as being a *reaction* to workers' struggles. It is important to keep in mind that the US labor movement before World War I—when Black slaves in the South did not yet have a role in the market as a free labor force—was the most powerful in the world, acted with an absolute principle of workers' autonomy, and used all the attributes of the proletariat against capital. This movement was outlawed, but its capacity to deal with capital was based on the fact that the Wobblies' leaders travelled constantly, did not have a fixed organization, and were not in any way institutionalized or involved in coalitions—they were the direct expression of workers' autonomy. They did not negotiate, sign contracts, or respect any particular agreements, given that they did not even make any agreements with the representatives of capital. At the entrance to the factory—i.e., where *they* were to be found—they wrote down the hours of work and the wages they expected on a piece of paper and gave it to the contractor. If he did not respect it, they did not work. Their principles were: internationalism and equality.

Again: the workers' struggles *before* World War I, as well as the mass strikes in Russia in 1905 and the miners' revolts in Germany, must be understood as the most radical uprising of labor against capital *within* the capitalist relationship—that is, being trapped in the contradiction arising from the process of the socialization of production within the emerging monopolies—thus, these struggles attained their explosive force by acting as a counter-movement to the capitalist process. What is important is that this strike movement was centered in the advanced industries. In Germany, the movement began among the miners and spread primarily to the chemical and electronics industries, industries that had already begun to export capital by the turn of the century. The socialization of production and the internationalization of capital are a single process.

Without dwelling explicitly on the notion of "the socialization of production," Lenin developed his model of the Bolshevik Party on the basis of the analysis and experience of these economic struggles, as a party—and this is important—to organize insurrection, arming the workers.

In Germany, the unions broke with the Social Democratic Party and thereby established the *separation* of political and economic struggles in the labor movement—a separation that also served the interests of capital.

The October Revolution was the culminating moment of a process that began with the class struggles of 1905, of workers' power, to which, with the party, Lenin had bestowed coherence, structure, and continuity—particularly as a result of his accurate appraisal of the role the war would play in the development of the insurgency.

On the other hand, the German Social Democrats not only agreed to the war credits in 1914 but also to the call for "disarmament" at the Zimmerwald Conference,[14] declaring pacifism to be the policy of the workers. This was certainly key to capital's use of the proletarian parties after World War I. During the war, it was the trade unions in the factories that organized the exploitation of labor for the war, the so-called war economy. As a result, after 1917–1918, the councils in Germany were very reluctant to organize. In any case, they were also incapable of organizing themselves, and—this is important—they advocated for a model of workers' autonomy and self-management that would be incapable

---

14   The September 1915 Zimmerwald Conference brought together a number of socialist factions that opposed World War I.

of overthrowing the labor/capital contradiction, the capitalist organization of production.

It was only with Roosevelt's New Deal in the early 1930s that Taylorism, as a method of dividing the proletariat through socialized production, was brought together with the social democratic organization of the proletariat, through state control of economic struggles, the institutionalization of contradictions, and social policies that anticipated class struggles in order to depoliticize them, and finally consumer culture—that is, the mass production of consumer goods facilitated by assembly-line production and higher wages at the price of the intensification of labor. Thus, Roosevelt's New Deal as a method of crisis management was understood as fascist in the economic sense (George insists that the organization of work in US industry is "fascist," and in this historical context this is entirely correct)[15] and social democratic in the state sense, i.e., in the organization and structuring of society by the state, through the creation of a dense network of government-created social institutions.

The New Deal, drawing on Bismarck's use of social legislation to undermine social democracy in the same way that the SPD used it after World War I to pacify the proletariat, became the state planning model that matched the form adopted in Germany by US capital after 1945—with the help of the SPD, which had been bought off, and Böckler's German Confederation of Trade Unions,[16] which was controlled by the CIA—creating and structuring a thoroughly anticommunist state.

As some Italian authors (who, in order to understand the class struggles in Italy in the early 1960s, studied developments in Germany after 1918 in much greater depth than any German group) categorically concluded, it is an error to speak of the SPD's politics after 1918, after the abolition of the monarchy, which was the only result of the council movement, as betrayal. That's not the point. In terms of the proletariat, from the October Revolution onward, social democracy became *the* most useful tool capital had at the state level and, by means of the trade unions, for the organization of anticommunism and for turning

---

15   George Jackson, *Blood in My Eye* (New York: Random House, 1972), 128f.
16   Hans Böckler was a Social Democratic deputy during the Weimar Republic. After 1945 he was president of the German Confederation of Trade Unions, having reorganized German trade unions with the support of US trade unions and having established the tripartite concertation system in the metalwork industry.

class struggle into an integral part of capital's development by depoliticizing it.

Thus, the *political* organization of labor through Taylorism, the division of the proletariat, the de-skilling of the labor force, and—most importantly—the establishment of a hierarchy in the factory and the total stultification of labor created a new layer of technocrats who controlled production as a technical matter and supervised workers accordingly, thereby structurally anticipating the fascist state's industrial police.

That is the contradiction in the layer of technicians, as pointed out by Gorz:[17] they are as dependent on their employer as the worker is, but because of their control function in relation to the workers they are immediate enemies of the working class. In May 1968, this contradiction was broadly resolved by this social stratum siding with the workers. However, following the collapse of the mass movement of 1968, they once again found themselves on the side of capital. As such, no combative workplace initiatives can be expected from them. Nonetheless, given their ambivalent position, they have revolutionary potential. At this point, there is nothing more to be said on the subject.

At the level of the state, social democratic policy as a means of dividing and atomizing the proletariat is in keeping with the counterrevolutionary project of capital since the October Revolution. Social democracy is the political expression of capital's interest in developing the relations of capital as relations of capital and, where that it is no longer possible, to freeze them by the penetration of society by the state, this being *the* anticommunist approach, which right up to the 1968 emergency laws was determined by the revolutionary model of the October Revolution.

The October Revolution, as the first breach in capitalist relations and a historical turning point, has served as a rebuke to capitalist development since 1917—since then, capitalist politics are both a *reaction* and an anticipation. As Brandt says:[18] "Stability is the anticipation of catastrophe in order to prevent it."

---

17   André Gorz, *Stratégie ouvrière et néocapitalisme* (Paris: Seuil, 1964).
18   Willy Brandt, former West German chancellor.

History of West Germany and the Old Left
Early May 1976

The following text was written for presentations to be delivered during the evidentiary motions at the Stammheim trial.

As part of the development of the imperialist world system under the hegemony of US capital and its politico-military expression—US foreign policy and its primary instrument, the US military—after 1945, the US established three states as operational bases for US foreign policy outside the US: West Germany, South Korea, and South Vietnam. From the outset, the role of these states for US imperialism was twofold: they were bases for US military operations to encircle and eventually roll back the Soviet Union and the Red Army, and they were operational bases for US capital to organize the Southeast and East Asian regions and Western Europe in its own interests.

We are interested in the history of West Germany for two reasons: we are, of course, interested in the history of the Old Left, the former opposition that was integrated and neutralized in 1966 with the entry of the Social Democrats into the Grand Coalition in Bonn.[19] We are also obviously interested in how revolutionary anti-imperialism and proletarian internationalism have been impacted by the role of West Germany in the global system of US capital: anticommunism and the political-economic-military subordination of Western Europe to US foreign policy—in other words, the direct line from Adenauer to Schmidt in West German government policy being a function of US global "domestic" policy[20]—that is, a function of the US's post-1945 role as the world's policeman.

---

19 The "Grand Coalition" of the CDU/CSU (Christian Democratic Union/Christian Social Union) and the SPD (Social Democratic Party), a federal government that was in power from December 1, 1966, to October 21, 1969, with Kurt Georg Kiesinger as chancellor and Willy Brandt as foreign minister and vice chancellor. It was followed by an SPD and FDP (Free Democratic Party) coalition from October 22, 1969, to May 7, 1974, with Willy Brandt as chancellor and Walter Scheel as foreign minister. At the time, Bonn was the West German capital.

20 Konrad Adenauer (Christian Democratic Union) was chancellor of West Germany from September 20, 1949, to October 11, 1963, followed by Ludwig Erhard (CDU) from October 17, 1963, to November 30, 1966. Helmut Schmidt (SPD) was chancellor of an SPD/FDP coalition from May 16, 1974, to October 1, 1982.

The fact that the domestic and foreign policies of South Korea and South Vietnam were clearly CIA policies is a predictable result of the economic weakness of the comprador bourgeoisie in neocolonial states.[21] The fact that a state with the economic potential of West Germany has had no political power or direction of its own for over thirty years is one of the reasons why it is particularly difficult to develop a radical political orientation in this state. As we have experienced, doing so can only be achieved through armed anti-imperialist struggle.

We don't know of any other country, and that's saying something, where the left so dismissively refuses to acknowledge its own history, which is certainly the history of its defeats, but that doesn't mean that the struggles it has waged have not been serious and are not worth studying. As we have already indicated, we have found that the Italians provide the most profound analyses of the politics of social democracy and its function *for* capital, while there are some really useful analyses from France of the Third Reich and German fascism's economic policy as the state policy of German monopoly capital. As for reflection on the major anti-imperialist mobilization against the US war in Vietnam in the capitalist centers in 1966–1967, it simply cannot be denied that the legal left has marketed it, consumed it, and made it the euphoric object of its memory but has never made the effort to come to grips with what really happened, where the student movement got its explosive power, the political relevance of its subjectivity, etc.

It was, however, entirely predictable, and it would appear that the experiences of the anticolonial revolutions—for example, those of the Algerian people, as they were introduced into the international discussions of the revolutionary left by Fanon[22]—are, in any case, applicable to West Germany, given its specific colonial status within the US state system. In the context of proletarian internationalism, the history of a people, in this case the history of Germany, and, as such, our history,

---

21 The dictatorships of Syngman Rhee and Park Chung-hee in South Korea and of Ngo Dinh Diem, Nguyen Cao Ky, and Nguyen Van Thieu in South Vietnam were established and maintained with the help of the CIA. See the June 1976 testimony by former CIA agent Philip Agee for the Stammheim trial (that was not admitted by the court): socialhistoryportal.org/raf/5541.

22 Frantz Fanon, *The Wretched of the Earth* (New York: Grove Press, 1963 [1961]); one of the most important books for revolutionary struggle in the twentieth century.

ceases to be a history that one should be ashamed of—which is the natural reaction of almost all communists to German history, at least since 1933, because the history of the Germans, of German monopoly capital, of German social democracy, of the trade unions, the history of the German workers' movement, is the history of failing to prevent two imperialist world wars and twelve years of fascism, of having failed to even resist it in a meaningful way. This is simply a fact that one cannot avoid when trying to develop a historical identity for the guerrilla here.

The history of Germany's Old Left is the history of its instrumentalization and, thus, neutralization by the Communist Party, as an appendage of the GDR,[23] and its corruption by social democracy, its symbolic figures—or, better, its public faces—being Brandt and Heinemann.[24]

The Old Left got to know Brandt when, in 1958, like all West Berlin mayors, in his capacity as a CIA-directed public figure, he made a tour of West Berlin's businesses and engaged in widespread anticommunist agitation, while putting himself at the helm of unrest on the factory floor with regard to Bonn's project to equip the West German army with nuclear arms, in order to take over and stifle the protests and give them anticommunist content.

The political *project* that the US, as the hegemonic occupying power in the three Western zones,[25] pursued reactively and defensively in the global setting, and offensively and *proactively* in its regional expression within the West German state, lacked legitimacy from the outset: the restoration of monopoly capital; the reconstruction of the old ruling economic and state elites to continue the dictatorship of the bourgeoisie, now under the command of US capital; remilitarization of the three Western zones and their integration into the US imperialist economic and military system at the cost of national unity; the continuity of anticommunism as the ruling ideology, as such, with the goal of German

---

23 GDR: the German Democratic Republic (or East Germany), part of the Soviet bloc.

24 Gustav Heinemann, representative of the radical democratic wing of German Protestantism. After a period of political wandering, he was an SPD member of the federal parliament from 1957 to 1969, minister of justice from 1966 to 1969, and president of the republic from 1969 to 1974. Willy Brandt was the mayor of West Berlin from 1957 to 1966, before joining the Kiesinger government in the federal parliament.

25 At the end of World War II, Germany was divided into four zones: an Eastern zone (*Ostzone*), a protectorate of the Soviet Union, and three Western zones, protectorates of the United States, France, and Great Britain respectively.

reunification being nothing but an opportunist calculation meant to politically neutralize the proletariat.

This policy was never up for discussion. It was not voted on in elections. It was decided in Washington. When elections were finally held in 1949, after the founding of the Federal Republic of Germany, the country's currency was already integrated into the Bretton Woods dollar system. To satisfy the needs of the Allies and the US, the parliamentary council furnished the state with a constitution in which the political direction was determined by a *single* figure, the chancellor—that is to say, the constitution of a puppet regime, if one takes the practice and reality of the Adenauer regime as the starting point and not the constitutional rationalizations about what had allegedly been learned from the Weimar Republic.[26]

Within the SPD, the power struggles in favor of Schumacher's anti-communism came to their conclusion[27]—now financed by US capital, the SPD resumed its old 1918 role as a bulwark against the influence of communists and against any attempt at workers' autonomy.[28] All key positions in the national executive committees of the trade unions and in the German Confederation of Trade Unions were occupied by the old bureaucrats who had already proven their value for capital and their capacity to integrate the class struggle on behalf of capital during the Weimar Republic. An initiative that attempted the obvious, to reconstruct the organizations of the proletariat from the clandestine groups that had joined the resistance against fascism, was smashed.

The specific function that West Germany has in the US imperialist state system, and, thus, in the strategy of US capital, is the product of its history as a counter-state founded by the US in the context of the East-West conflict. This also explains the specific role of the SPD in the US strategy in Vietnam.

---

26 "What had allegedly been learned from the Weimar Republic" is an ironic reference to the legislative measures of successive West German governments to avoid the polarization of society "between left-wing and right-wing extremists."

27 Kurt Schumacher, chairman of the SPD from 1945 to 1952.

28 The November Revolution of 1918, at the end of World War I, was suppressed with the help of the SPD under the leadership of Friedrich Ebert, Philip Scheidemann, and Gustav Noske. As such, the SPD bears direct responsibility for the massacre of the Spartacists and the assassination of their leaders Rosa Luxemburg, Karl Liebknecht, and Leo Jogiches at the hand of paramilitaries acting under direct government orders.

The historical roots of West Germany's role, as the second strongest member of NATO and as a state with the most far-reaching ambitions in terms of imperialist politics after the US, lie in its continuity with the Third Reich and in the fact that German monopoly capital has always had to be extremely aggressive, because of its structure and extreme dependency on the world market, i.e., on exports.

As such, it is understandable that no opposition movement in West Germany prior to the student movement received even the slightest response in parliament, because all opposition movements were taken over and stifled by social democracy. The special infamy of the SPD, first and foremost, is to have always been the revisionist party of the proletariat and, as such, to have always acted as the agent of capital within the proletariat, today totally guided by directives from Clay in Berlin,[29] from the CIA, from the Pentagon, etc.

The process undertaken by the SPD: adapting its official political line to official US foreign policy. Just like the CDU aimed at destroying the opposition movements that continued to exist until around 1960: movements against remilitarization, against fascists in the state apparatus, against the integration of West Germany into NATO, against equipping the army with nuclear weapons. Until Wehner,[30] in 1960, anticipating the Grand Coalition, openly declared the Social Democrats' commitment to NATO, to the integration of the Federal Republic of Germany into the West, and to the goals of Adenauer's *Ostpolitik*,[31] i.e., rollback. This was nothing but a signal to US foreign policy that the SPD had carried out its postwar mission: to absorb and destroy the legal opposition in West Germany.

The special dependence of West German imperialism on US capital is characterized not only by the fact that, like capital in all the other states in the US bloc, it is dominated by the US and, as such, the West German state is obliged to adapt politically and institutionally to the conditions of reproduction of hegemonic capital; the special element is that this state's political leadership has never controlled its own

---

29 Lucius Clay, military governor of the US zone, based in West Berlin.
30 Herbert Wehner, chairman of the SPD parliamentary group from 1966 to 1974.
31 Konrad Adenauer's "*Ostpolitik*" (Eastern policy) toward the GDR (East Germany) consisted of refusing to recognize the GDR in the hope that it would collapse through the exodus of its inhabitants attracted by the "magnet" of the West.

constitutional institutions. As a result, it functions as an expression of US "domestic" policy.

From the beginning, this was not only a matter of the rules of occupation. It was institutional strategy: after 1945, US capital did more than simply restructure West Germany's constitution.

In its operational elements—a chancellor-based democracy, a parliament limited in its jurisdiction by a system based on a federation of states, the repurposing of the fascist civil service in both the republic's judiciary and its administration—it has taken control of all the other institutions that make up the imperialist state: parties, business associations, trade unions, and the mass media.

It could be said that when it came to confrontations in West Germany there has been a lack of clarity about the actual power relations, so much so that prior to the student movement class conflicts in West Germany had no political dimension at all, they had the character of sham conflicts that could be described as shadow boxing.

To provide an example: the anti-nuclear movement developed around the debate in the German parliament in March 1958, following the controversy in February in which Heinemann and Dehler[32] opposed Adenauer's reunification policy and Stalin's offer in 1952 and 1955 to allow Western-style elections in the GDR as part of a neutral Germany. The movement's starting point was the federal parliament's decision to equip the West German army with delivery systems that could be used for weapons armed with nuclear warheads. It hardly entered the consciousness of this movement that this decision was nothing but the ratification of a NATO decision, i.e., a Pentagon decision.

This is an example of the governmental structure developed on the basis of West Germany's status as a defeated and occupied country, whereby the relevant decision-making processes are adapted to an institutional strategy from which democratic choice is removed or can be removed as a decisive or even partial factor of power, as a result of the military domination of politics.

It is clear that this state could only serve its current function for US capital as a result of the particular role played by West German social democracy.

---

32 Thomas Dehler, minister of justice in the first Adenauer government.

By 1960, for example, the old extra-parliamentary left—which had resisted the process of the country's East-West division, rearmament and integration into NATO, and the policy of reclaiming the so-called Eastern German territories—was paralyzed. The trade union opposition, especially in the IG-Metall,[33] where the part of the SDS that had been purged from the SPD could still find a basis for growth, fell apart in the following years under the impact of the emergency laws against the protests of the democratic left;[34] or, rather, it allowed itself to get ground down in this process. While the SPD continued to act as a mouthpiece for criticism of the government's positions—the deployment of the West German army inside the country, the crushing of strikes, the suspension of parliament, the total mobilization of the population in the event of a state of emergency,[35] etc.—its material content was drained through the wrangling of constitutional experts, and in this way the opposition was ultimately deprived of its mass base. In this case, the result was also paralysis, using the old social democratic trick of institutionalizing struggles in public hearings, where everything unfolded as the purview of experts and where the question of power was eliminated.

In short, in the final analysis, what makes social democracy suitable as a tool for US capital is, in one word: demagogy.

October Revolution—The Third International
From the discussion in Stammheim, early May 1976

We have said that the October Revolution determined the structure of the reactionary process in the West—meaning, the development of capital became an explicitly *political* process tied to the international relationship between revolution and imperialism.

Second, it effectively produced the military-political East-West demarcation line through a protracted and painful process of Soviet accumulation.

---

33 IG-Metall, metalworkers' union, one of the most important unions in West Germany at the time.
34 SDS, Socialist German Students' Federation; see the Chronology at the end of this volume.
35 The emergency laws were passed by the federal parliament in May 1968.

The third factor was the liberation struggles of the peoples of the Third World.[36] These found their revolutionary starting point here, in that they were able to organize themselves internationally within the Third International, which had been established as a result of the October Revolution. Meaning that they could raise their struggle to the *political* level that proletarian politics requires in order to be effective.

This was one of Lenin's central theses for the organization of the world revolutionary process at the first (or second?) congress of the Third International. It's in that awful Comintern book we have—look it up or give it to me if you have it—well, otherwise, I might forget, shit[37]—that the revolution *must* operate, from the first moment, at the political *level* of the counterrevolutionary process, and that if it fails to anticipate the level of the counterrevolution in its initiative, it anticipates its defeat. Or, in other words: it *must* fail.

Defending the conquest of power in one country, the October Revolution, and the organization of the world revolutionary process were *a single* thing for Lenin.

The Russian Revolution cannot be properly addressed without noting that an essential aspect of Lenin's concept of internationalism was his understanding of revolutionary morality, i.e., his precise understanding that "serving the people" meant serving the international proletariat. He meant this not only for himself: on this basis, he determined the domestic process in Russia before and after the October Revolution as an *instrument* of the world revolutionary process—as effectively subordinated to this process. We mention this in passing, because a large part of the narrow nationalist left still references Lenin, and Lenin quotes play a role in the revisionist left's agitation against the RAF's internationalism. In the meantime, the aversion the non-revisionist left has developed for Lenin, at least as they imagine him, which they confuse for reality, has little or nothing to do with what Lenin actually did and what he fought for in the international communist movement: proletarian internationalism.

---

36   Third World not in the sense of the dependent "Global South" but as a designation of those countries' anti-imperialist struggle.

37   In fact, Lenin's theses can be found among his interventions during the second and third congresses of the Communist International; V.I. Lenin, *Collected Works*, vols. 31 and 32 (Moscow: Progress Publishers, 1964/1965).

Of course, the historical falsifications in the Moscow Institute of Science's Marx/Engels publications are also part of that. But as I said previously, here we are not interested in the theoretical reception of Lenin but in the real process that was initiated by the October Revolution and the Third International.

Marxist orthodoxy was and, it must be said, still is a *white* phenomenon. Thus, in its criticism and analyses of the politics of the Third International, the conscious role the International played in the development of the anticolonial revolutions in East Asia is absent. (If it were not, the image of Stalin would have to be reconsidered, because on the colonial question Stalin was an ultraleft Leninist, and the Stalin/Hitler equivalency does not hold water. So it is necessary to dispense with that, or use it to criticize the MLs and analyze the continuity between anticommunism and their politics against social imperialism. These little piglets lay claim to Stalin—or what?—what do you say, Gudrun?— or to Stalinism and China's foreign policy.)[38]

Schlesinger says, "As to the power and political support that the Russian Revolution could provide to the colonial revolutions, and had to provide for reasons of mere self-preservation, it was irrelevant how the recipients assessed the Russian Revolution itself" and "The issue of a revolution's isolation was no longer an issue for the colonial countries, since the support of the Soviet Union was a given."[39]

When, today, Brandt uses the Socialist International to organize social democracy's counterrevolutionary project[40]—its development project as a project for subjugating the states in the US state system to

---

38 At the Stammheim trial, the four had already made their views on Soviet and Chinese foreign policy clear in a text by Gudrun Ensslin, "Stück zur Sowjetunion," January 19, 1976, https://socialhistoryportal.org/raf/5505.

39 Rudolf Schlesinger, *Die Kolonialfrage in der Kommunistischen Internationale* (Hamburg: EVA, 1970); Schlesinger was a member of the KPD, editor of the German Comintern publications, and co-founder of the Institute for Soviet and East European Studies in Glasgow. Translation by the editors.

40 After the fall of the fascist regimes in the Mediterranean countries, the SPD intervened through its foundation, the Friedrich Ebert Stiftung, and its contacts in the US to train pro-NATO political cadres. The SPD also played a leading role in the Socialist International, a worldwide organization of social democratic parties that seek to establish "democratic socialism," understood to be in opposition to communist movements. In 2013, the SPD, the British Labour Party and the Progressive Alliance of Social Democratic Parties in the European Parliament reduced their participation in the Socialist International, pushing for its "reform," meaning the exclusion of members they consider to be "too radical."

the US capitalist development model, capital investment at the cost of national sovereignty, doing so concretely in the case of Greece, Turkey, Spain, and Portugal and with ties to NATO in the case of Yugoslavia—it is necessary to keep in mind that this party[41] has its roots in the Second International, whose position on the colonial question has been unequivocal and always racist and chauvinist, always in favor of imperialist exploitation and opposed to the liberation of peoples that was represented by the Third International.

It is the revisionist left that invokes Lenin, and the anti-revisionist left that rejects him. It is important to remember that Lenin's theory of imperialism and his theory of the role of the state after the conquest of power by the proletariat were developed in opposition to social democracy, in opposition to the Zimmerwald Conference,[42] and in opposition to the Second International—and from the standpoint of the international proletariat, insofar as Lenin was clearly on the side of the Third World liberation movements against imperialism.

Lenin's approach was not based on or in support of an abstract theoretical position. The core of all Lenin's thinking was oriented toward the organization of insurrection in a global framework; that is, the organization of the armed struggle against imperialism. It is a dirty little bit of opportunism to present Lenin's writing on left radicalism as his key text—this text targets the kind of left communism that today finds its caricature in the Sponti left,[43] for which the international dimension of the revolutionary struggle does not exist any more than it does for any of the other sects. Also: How is it possible that a KBW guy lets himself get shot in Portugal while working at an agricultural commune,[44] rather than fighting in the underground against the system here—a system that, at the same time, can also shoot at workers in Portugal, which is particularly clear, given what happened in Chile with clockwork precision.

---

41 Meaning the SPD, the Social Democratic Party of Germany.
42 The September 1915 Zimmerwald Conference brought together a number of socialist groups that opposed World War I.
43 The "Spontis" were part of the German autonomist left at the time. The text by Lenin being referred to here is "'Left-Wing' Communism: an Infantile Disorder" (April–May 1920) in *Collected Works*, vol. 31 (Moscow: Progress Publishers, 1964), 17–118.
44 KBW, one of the self-styled Marxist-Leninist groups active at the time.

The Third International organized the communist parties in preparation for armed struggle, and they eventually played that role in the peasant revolutions in China and Indochina. The Communist Parties of Korea and Indonesia, under the protection of the Communist International, organized the anticolonial revolution. While the communist parties in Latin America, being the product of Eurocentric intellectuals, failed to reach the Latin American base, i.e., the Indigenous population.

The Third International—and this is the key thing—was anti-white, so if you're wondering where the Soviet Union gets its prestige in the Third World—besides, of course, by supplying arms to the liberation movements—it is due to the historical continuity of those politics.

In retrospect, the Chinese attempt in the early 1960s to present the Sino-Soviet conflict as a conflict between white communism and the communism of the black, yellow, red, etc. populations in Latin America, Africa, and Asia was China's attempt to usurp the powerful tradition of the Third International in order to stifle it. Specifically, Chinese foreign policy does not organize the liberation movements of people of color against imperialism but neutralizes them and goes so far as to support reactionary regimes like that of Mrs. Bandaranaike in Ceylon (Sri Lanka) against the liberation movements, called "Guevarists" by reactionaries, for whose destruction counterinsurgency equipment is being provided—helicopters, etc.

Well, in any case, this piece might accompany a piece on the MLs, etc.—where there would be more to say about Chinese foreign policy.

As such, there are, I think, two lines: first—the three development models: the Chinese model, which neutralizes the independent states in the North-South front and, as such, serves the interests of imperialist politics; the Soviet model: developing heavy industry/non-simultaneity[45]/support for armed struggle; the social democratic model: economic aid plus counterinsurgency. Put differently: the Chinese development model neutralizes the anti-imperialist struggle, the Soviet

---

45   "Non-simultaneity" or "uneven political and economic development": a principle often analyzed by Lenin, introduced in 1915 in his article "On the Slogan for a United States of Europe," in *Collected Works*, vol. 21 (Moscow: Progress Publishers, 1964), 343. Developed further in V.I. Lenin, "Imperialism, the Highest Stage of Capitalism," in *Collected Works*, vol. 22 (Moscow: Progress Publishers, 1964), 185ff.

model supports the anti-imperialist struggle, and the social democratic model organizes the counterrevolution

—second, "white communism."

We'll see.

Andreas and Ulrike's Reflections on Another Upcoming Trial
April 1976

What is happening is that social democracy is organizing the reactionary process in Western Europe by means of the enormous economic potential of West German imperialism under the hegemony of US capital, which controls *all* the strategic industries in West Germany: electronics, chemical, oil, automobile, mechanical engineering. This reactionary process is organized on two levels, with the social democratic development model serving as the means: credits that come with political conditions and whose function it is to prepare for capital investments by imposing the militarization of politics via economic blackmail—Brandt: "Stability is the anticipation of catastrophe in order to prevent it" (in a letter to Olaf Palme).[46]

Economic blackmail is used to compel states subordinate to Germany in the imperialist chain to adopt its model of fascism: institutional strategy, counterinsurgency, and the organization of the state using the parliamentary democratic model, while marginalizing the communist parties, so that the only ruling bloc *possible* is one that supports US capital.

Within Western Europe, German social democracy is the main enemy representing the US, because it alone has the tools required for the new fascism, as a result of its history, of its control of the Socialist International, and of its contacts in the state-run trade unions and parties that still retain some connection with their base.

The reality is that *every* attack on the presence of US capital here *is* immediately confronted by the imperialist state or—as was discussed in 1972—directly by US military forces. In *any* case, attacks on US

---

46 Willy Brandt and Olaf Palme were leading social democrats in West Germany and Sweden respectively.

installations here force the state to show its true face as a tool of US capital *and* as institutional camouflage for Germany's true status in the US state system: a territory militarily occupied by the US.

That is *also* a line of mobilization. However, what is essential is that exposing social democracy through the attacks of small armed groups will make it impossible for it to organize Western Europe as a military power bloc for this US strategy, because exposing it here will necessarily energize all of the political resentment for West Germany that exists abroad—among old antifascists and in all groups across the spectrum from the far left to the social democrats, as well as in the national governments—the resentment against the Germans, German imperialism, German militarism, and German hegemonic aspirations, specifically along a line that recognizes that the main enemy is the US, and, thus, that the first line of demarcation—the *front*—is the North-South conflict, the liberation struggles of the peoples of the Third World: the world proletariat vs. the US.

What is at issue is developing the second line of demarcation in the capitalist centers, which is determined by the repercussions of the liberation struggles at the system's periphery on the capitalist centers—ideologically, politically, militarily, and *economically* (which we will not develop further here)—as part of the *front*, part of the military-political confrontation, a process by which the guerrilla in the capitalist centers *becomes* a part of the Third World liberation struggle, i.e., part of the vanguard of the world proletariat.

That, in short, is the strategy we have in mind based on our experience and on what we have learned so far. The line: forcing capital and its state to respond to the onslaught of small revolutionary groups, to *react*. In this way the second front (which we want) will set in motion a process of polarization as a result of the persecution of the left, etc., in which the guerrilla can be, and we say will be, seen to represent everyone who understands their problems *politically* (as opposed to privately—which is the case for the Sponti scene, generally speaking).

There is also something to say about the organizational structure/composition of the urban guerrilla that fights on this front, but we will leave that aside here.

So it is necessary to analyze the role of social democracy in the US military project: the integration of the apparatuses of internal and external security—the transformation of the entire state apparatus, including schools, the media, and all of the administrative institutions into a giant intelligence-gathering arm of the intelligence services by obliging all civil servants and employees to pass on information to the Verfassungsschutz (in accordance with, e.g., the Lower Saxony Intelligence Services Act, which has only been examined in *one* West German newspaper, Spoo in the *Frankfurter Rundschau*).[47]

The institutional strategy of the new fascism is to make the political judiciary an arm of the political police—the simultaneous expansion of the state security machine: the BKA, and within the BKA the Terrorism Department (TE) in Bonn, the BGS, the MEK,[48] the riot police, the unification of the state police forces under the command of the BKA, computerization and the new repressive technologies used and analyzed for psychological warfare.

It is vertically and horizontally (within Western Europe) directed; i.e., it is intra-state and inter-state, and geared toward creating an intelligence-oriented military apparatus that penetrates societies and integrates states, without having a political expression of its own; which is to say: it is totally beyond public control and under the command of the Pentagon. It is a military machine that is simultaneously a propaganda apparatus for total manipulation as an aspect of psychological warfare.

Insofar as the system of intelligence gathering and output as psychological warfare becomes a closed system, manipulation and control and, thus, patterns of constantly renewed manipulation can and do develop, multiply, and evolve. In this context, there is, of course, a reality that the legal left does not understand at all, which is that they already have files in the BKA computer, about both themselves and their circle of acquaintances and friends, as well as the contents of their address books, which were confiscated during the "Winterreise" raids,[49]

---

47 The Verfassungsschutz is the German internal intelligence service at both the federal and state levels. Eckart Spoo was a journalist whose articles appeared in a number of dailies, including the *Frankfurter Rundschau*.

48 Various repressive agencies: the BKA-TE (responsible for both the hunt for RAF members and for determining prisoners' transport and detention conditions), the BGS (the border police, including the special intervention unit, the GSG-9), the MEK (local police intervention units, similar to American SWAT teams).

49 Aktion Winterreise (Operation Winter Journey) was a wave of raids coordinated by the federal police on November 24, 1974, targeting alleged RAF sympathizers. Publications were seized from publishers, printers, and bookshops, and a number of journalists, publishers, and booksellers were arrested.

and any other information that has been systematically collected since 1966–1967 at the latest.

Just to be clear: if the BKA can capture 394 gun collectors in a coordinated action, it could, of course, transport the entire legal left to stadiums in a single action.[50]

The urban guerrilla is a tactic that indicates the strategy by anticipating it: the international reconstruction of proletarian politics and, thus, the response based on international conditions. In terms of strategizing revolutionary politics, this means understanding the national state as an apparatus of domestic repression that is internationally determined by transnational US capital.

The system of national states within the US imperialist state system is a system of sectors of the front in the war waged by US capital's repressive apparatus at the points where two lines of demarcation crystallize: rich and poor in the North-South conflict and a second line of demarcation within the capitalist centers, in anticipation of mass proletarian counterviolence.

As such, it is important to note that the capitalist state acts on the basis of constraints imposed on it by the movement of capital, the material basis of the whole affair. This is one function of capital. At the same time, capital is no longer able to develop a productive perspective on its own. Or, to use an expression from bourgeois economics: it is no longer capable of innovation once it ceases to be the subject of the social reproduction of state activity.

For a figure like Schmidt, it is clear that if it cannot solve the problem of the economy, of the crisis, of inflation, of unemployment, in a word, the problem of the world market, the imperialist state system is a giant with feet of clay.

What is new about this fascism, however, is that it is not only concerned with securing the rule of capital, the markets, and its own consolidation but also with the formation of a state system that can assert itself independent of its base and the constraints of the movement of capital.

---

50 The reference to "stadiums": when Pinochet came to power in a CIA-backed coup d'état in Chile in 1973, tens of thousands of leftists and suspected leftists were quickly rounded up and interned in sports stadiums that were converted into prison camps, where many were tortured and killed.

In this case, the state determines the policies and is no longer governed by competing factions of capital but is the direct expression of capital, because under the hegemony of US capital there is no economic, and, thus, no political, autonomy for any faction of capital vis-à-vis US capital.

What is important for us here is to expose how the dialectic of the internationalization of the movement of capital transforms the individual states within the US imperialist state system into a new, internationally organized fascism; that is to say, the new role of the state based on the constraints imposed by imperialism's being on the strategic defensive following its defeat in Vietnam.

The key thing we are interested in clarifying is that, given that repression is internationally organized, revolutionary strategy *must* also be internationalist, which is to say that the political-economic analysis of the current situation coincides with the Marxist concept, concretely meaning the strategy outlined in *The Communist Manifesto*: "Workers of the world unite." This has found its organizational expression in the guerrilla, which anticipates the internationalist reconstruction of proletarian politics. The guerrilla will be the organizational form of proletarian internationalism in the capitalist centers.

A Few Words About Röhl

Late 1975

This text was released by the prisoners and was part of the documenta-
tion distributed on May 18, 1977, by the International Committee for the
Defense of Political Prisoners in Western Europe (IVK, formed in Paris
on December 14, 1974, with sections in West Germany, France, Italy,
Holland, Belgium, and England) in order to provide some facts to coun-
ter a smear campaign against the founding members of the RAF. We are
publishing it here because the clichés, projections, and slanders used
in the psychological warfare against the RAF and especially against
Ulrike were largely based on Röhl's fantasies and his desire for revenge.

What follows are a few words about Röhl in response to the social
democratic faction of the intelligence services trumpeting his new
novel in the *Frankfurter Rundschau* as if it were a book overflowing
with revelations.[1] It reveals nothing about us but quite a bit about cooperation between the SPD and the CIA and the corruption of the DKP.[2]

The book was published at the same time as Röhl's admission into
the SPD and his pornographic peddling at Molden Publishers. In terms

---

1   In 1975, Klaus Rainer Röhl, Ulrike's ex-husband, published *Die Genossin* (The Comrade),
    a novel about her, released by Molden Publishing, Vienna. The *Frankfurter Rundschau*
    is a leading German daily newspaper.
2   The connection between the SPD and the CIA has been documented on a number of
    occasions, especially since the party's involvement in the repression of the April 1974
    Carnation Revolution in Portugal. The DKP (German Communist Party) was founded
    in 1968 to circumvent the 1956 ban on the KPD (Communist Party of Germany), the
    party that had emerged from the Spartacus League in December 1918.

of publicity, Molden is the CIA and Pentagon's most important publishing instrument in Western Europe. Fritz Molden is the son-in-law of Allen Dulles, former head of the CIA, who in turn was the brother of John Foster Dulles—and it is well established that family ties mean something in intelligence circles (for example, the Diem clan in South Vietnam).

In 1965, Molden published the book *The Green Berets*, 4.5 million copies of which were distributed by the Pentagon in all the world's languages. In terms of publicity, *The Green Berets* was the Pentagon's key psychological action to condition international public opinion for the US escalation and "special war" against the Vietnamese people. With *The Green Berets*—as is the case for the Molden project with the Röhl book—the Pentagon pursued a policy of brutally assaulting world opinion. In the case of Vietnam in the mid-sixties, they didn't even try to sell freedom and democracy as war aims but simply pushed for a war of extermination against the people of Vietnam.

Röhl himself says that Simmel was his model and inspiration[3]—thus, shilling anticommunist trash and psychological warfare as a form of counterrevolutionary policy.

The purpose of the book is to provide the state security apparatus with a context for justifying the liquidation of Andreas. That is exactly how the *Frankfurter Rundschau* understood it—that there are gaps in Andreas's life story (which is as false as Kuby's description of Andreas in *Stern*).[4] In that sense, the disgusted literary critics who have torn this book apart are ignoring its political dimension, because this project is not about literary ambitions but about psychological warfare directed by the Pentagon, through the CIA's Molden Publishers, with input from the psychiatrist Hacker,[5] as can be seen from the clichés used. In this project, we once again see the essence of social democratic politics since 1945: the venality and the dependence on the CIA.

I would say that the editorial staff of the former *konkret*[6]—whose collaboration with the outlawed KPD was, in fact, the only possible radical opposition during the Cold War—has logically and consequently

---

3   Johannes Mario Simmel, novelist and journalist working with the weekly *Quick*.
4   Erich Kuby, journalist working with the weekly *Stern*, as well as other publications.
5   Friedrich Hacker, an aspiring psychiatric expert on aggression and terrorism.
6   *konkret*, a political magazine founded by Klaus Rainer Röhl in 1957. See Moncourt and Smith, 26 and 28, and the Chronology at the end of this volume.

become polarized over the last ten years, following the rupture that occurred in the mid-1960s and the important development that occurred within the political opposition in the form of the mobilization against the US war in Vietnam. It polarized the Old Left between two possibilities regarding the Third World liberation struggles in the context of the East-West relationship: Röhl ended up with the CIA, and I ended up in the urban guerrilla.

Röhl remained the corrupt and opportunistic pig he always was, and I freed myself from the corruption of bourgeois journalism.

This was an inevitable development, because no room remains for political opposition between integration, corruption, and instrumentalization by the CIA, on the one hand, and armed struggle from the underground and active participation in the organization of insurrection against the capitalist relations of production, on the other—because political opposition and clandestine struggle have become the same thing.

An Account of Giovanni Cappelli's Visit

May 7, 1976

Two days before her death, Ulrike received a visit from Giovanni Cappelli, a lawyer from Milan who was active in the International Committee for the Defense of Political Prisoners in Western Europe (IVK) and was a defense counsel in the trials against members of the Red Brigades. Her account of the visit is the last document we have from her.

Spazzali, Cappelli's partner, is the brother of the one who was arrested.

The interview was conducted in English, and the cops' translator only translated a few things, roughly speaking.

Cappelli said that the prisoners from the Red Brigades would like to correspond with us. We should write to them. I said that we can only correspond with our families. They are not isolated, only continually transferred but fully integrated, and they can work, etc. Their policy is to politicize the prisoners and the prison conditions. He said that a lot is happening at this level in Italy.

The only one who is isolated—that is to say, held alone in a cell and not, as is the norm, in a group of three—is Curcio.[1] He said it was for security reasons, because Curcio has already escaped once, and yesterday three other prisoners escaped. The lawyers are trying to get him out of solitary confinement, but these escapes will make that more

---

[1] Renato Curcio, one of the founders of the Red Brigades; see Renato Curcio, *A viso aperto* (Milan: Mondadori, 1993).

difficult. I got carried away, but he agreed that both there and here the security argument is just a smoke screen.

Twenty-four prisoners will be charged in the trial at the end of May. He says that the accusation addresses the overall Red Brigades policy from 1971–1972 to 1974. This will be the first major trial against the Red Brigades. The approach taken by the prosecution to laying charges in trials against the Red Brigades is to always address their overall practice during an entire period as an integrated whole.[2]

I asked him if he expected NATO to intervene in Italy if the Communist Party scored an electoral victory. He thought that would be absurd, as the PCI is a law and order party and is, therefore, implicated in the repression.

About the role of Germany in Europe he said: "representative" of the US; intervention would take place through the state apparatus. The function of the reactionary integration of Western Europe for the counterrevolution in the Third World and, in general, the relationship between the struggle in the capitalist centers and the development of the front in the Third World—he seemed taken aback when I spoke to him about it. He wanted to know if a broad socialist movement was still possible here, and, if so: Why isn't there one? In response, I explained the post-fascist state, the role of social democracy, the total dependence on the US, the total control of public opinion by the reactionary media, etc. He said that the role of Stammheim as a model, including for the political judiciary in Italy, was clear to them.

He took a few notes. He said it was so he could explain to his colleagues what I had said. I told him that if they ever wanted to publish anything we had talked about, they should show it to us first, and that they should not publish anything that had not been authorized by us. He replied that that was self-evident.

---

2   On April 17, 1976, the first major trial against the historical core of the Red Brigades began in Turin; see Mario Moretti, *Brigate rosse. Una storia italiana* (Milan: Anabasi, 1994).

Jan Raspe on Ulrike's Death

May 11, 1976

I don't have much to say.

We believe Ulrike was executed. We don't know how, but we know by whom, and we understand the reasoning behind the method. I recall Herold's statement, "Actions against the RAF must primarily be developed in such a way as to undermine the positions held by sympathizers."

And Buback: "State security is given life by those who are committed to it. People like Herold and myself, we always find a way."[1]

It was a cold, calculated execution, just like with Holger, just like with Siegfried Hausner. If Ulrike had decided to die, because she would have seen this as her last chance to save herself—to save her revolutionary identity—from the slow destruction of a person's will in the agony of isolation—then she would have told us—or at least she would have told Andreas: *that was the nature of their relationship to one another.*

I believe that the execution of Ulrike now, at this moment, can be understood in the light of the culmination and first political breakthrough in the conflict between the international guerrilla and the imperialist state of West Germany. There is information that points in this direction that I don't want to talk about now.

The murder is consistent with all of the state's attempts to deal with us over the past six years—the physical *and* moral destruction of the RAF—and it is aimed at all guerrilla groups in West Germany, for whom Ulrike played an essential ideological role.

---

1   Horst Herold, head of the BKA; Siegfried Buback, attorney general.

What still needs to be said—

As long as I've been witness to the relationship between Ulrike and Andreas—and I've known them for the past seven years—it was marked by intensity and tenderness, sensitivity, and clarity. And I believe that it was precisely because of this relationship that Ulrike was able to survive the eight months in the silent wing. It was a relationship like that which can develop between siblings, oriented around a common objective, as a function of this policy.

And, thus, it was free, because freedom is only possible in the struggle for liberation.

There was no breakdown in their relationship during these years. Such a thing wouldn't have been possible, because it was determined by the RAF's politics. And when there were any fundamental contradictions within the group, they were defined by concrete practice. Rooted in the identical situation of the struggle and the history of the group, there was no basis for them in the theoretical work process, which is the only work possible in prison.

That it was like this can be clearly seen in the discussions and Ulrike's letters and manuscripts up to Friday evening. They reflect the real character of this relationship.

It is a crude and sinister smear, a bid to use Ulrike's execution for psychological warfare purposes, to now claim that "tensions" and "estrangement" existed between Ulrike and Andreas, between Ulrike and us.[2] This is Buback in all his stupidity.

So far none of these attempts has led to anything but an ever clearer understanding of the reaction in West Germany as fascism.

---

2   In 2009, records surfaced showing that the head of the BKA had developed "Principles of Disinformation to Combat Terrorism" in October 1975. At a meeting with other state security agencies, one of the methods proposed was to "suggest and encourage conflicts between gang members," specifically mentioning the names Andreas Baader and Ulrike Meinhof. According to *Der Spiegel* (April 10, 2009), the BKA, with the help of the Attorney General and the Baden-Württemberg Ministry of the Interior circulated falsified letters after Ulrike's death to make it appear that there was tension between the prisoners in Stammheim, in order to dispel doubts about the suicide story. The psychological-pathological clichés used in these letters, as in the "psychograms" disseminated by BKA agent Alfred Klaus, were concocted by Klaus Rainer Röhl and his friends, including Stefan Aust, and continue to be repeated to this day by people who prefer lies to facts.

Communiqué from the Ulrike Meinhof Commando

April 13, 1977

For "protagonists of the system" like Buback, history always finds a way.

On April 7, 1977, the Ulrike Meinhof Commando executed Attorney General Siegfried Buback.

Buback was directly responsible for the murders of Holger Meins, Siegfried Hausner, and Ulrike Meinhof. In his function as attorney general—as the central figure connecting and coordinating matters between the justice system and the West German intelligence services, in close cooperation with the CIA and the NATO Security Committee—he stage-managed and directed their murders.

Under Buback's direction, Holger was intentionally murdered on November 9, 1974, by systematic undernourishment and the conscious manipulation of the transportation schedules from Wittlich to Stammheim. The AGO calculated that they could use the execution of a cadre to break the prisoners' collective hunger strike against the deadly prison conditions, after the attempt to kill Andreas by stopping the force-feeding failed due to the mobilization of public pressure.

Under Buback's direction, Siegfried, who had led the Holger Meins Commando and who could have proven that it was the West German intervention units who detonated the explosives at the West German embassy in Stockholm, was murdered on May 4, 1975. While he was completely in the hands of the AGO and the BKA, he was transferred to West Germany and subjected to a life-threatening transfer to the prison of Stuttgart-Stammheim, thereby assuring his death.

Under Buback's command, Ulrike was executed in a state security operation on May 9, 1976. Her death was staged as a suicide to make the politics that Ulrike had struggled for seem senseless.

The murder was an escalation, following the AGO's attempt to render Ulrike a cretin through a forced neuro-surgical operation, after which she was to be presented—destroyed—at the Stammheim trial, so as to condemn armed resistance as an illness. This project was prevented by international protests.

The timing of her murder was precisely calculated:

- before the decisive initiative in the trial, with defense motions that would have interpreted the 1972 RAF attacks against the US Headquarters in Frankfurt and Heidelberg in light of West Germany's participation in the US's aggression, contrary to international law, in Vietnam;

- before Ulrike was to be called as a witness in the Düsseldorf trial against the Holger Meins Commando, where she would have testified about the extreme form of torture that she had been subjected to for eight months in the silent wing;

- before her sentencing—because the critical international public opinion, which had developed as a result of the Stammheim show trial and the cynical use of imperialist violence, was acknowledged by the federal government and its executive organs and was about to rebound against the state.

Ulrike's history, in a way that is clearer than that of many combatants, is the history of the continuity of resistance. For the revolutionary movement, she embodied an ideological vanguard function, against which Buback's showpiece, the simulated suicide: her death—used in the AGO's propaganda as the "acknowledgement of the failure" of armed politics—was directed at morally destroying the group, its struggle, and its impact. The AGO's approach, which it has followed since 1971, with manhunts and operations conducted against the RAF, follows the counterinsurgency strategy of the NATO Security Committee: criminalization of revolutionary resistance—for which the tactical steps are infiltration, disrupting solidarity, isolating the guerrilla, and eliminating its leadership.

In the context of West Germany's imperialist counterstrategy, the justice system is an instrument of war—used to pursue the guerrilla operating underground and to exterminate the prisoners of war.

Buback—whom Schmidt called "an energetic combatant" for this state—understood the conflict with us as a war and engaged in it as such: "I have lived through the war. This is a war with different means."

We will prevent the AGO from murdering our fighters in West German prisons, which it intends to do simply because the prisoners will not stop struggling and the AGO has no solution other than their liquidation.

We will prevent the AGO and the state security services from retaliating against the imprisoned fighters for the actions of the guerrilla outside.

We will prevent the AGO from using the prisoners' fourth collective hunger strike for minimum human rights as an opportunity to murder Andreas, Gudrun, and Jan, which their psychological warfare has been openly promoting since Ulrike's death.

Organize the armed resistance and the anti-imperialist front in Western Europe.
Wage war in the capitalist centers as part of the international war of liberation.

—Ulrike Meinhof Commando—Red Army Faction

Chronology

October 7, 1934
Ulrike is born.

1955–1957
Ulrike studies philosophy and education and takes courses in psychology, German literature, English literature, art history, and historical sciences at the University of Marburg.

August 17, 1956
The Communist Party of Germany (KPD) is banned.

1957–1959
Ulrike studies education, philosophy, psychology, and art history at the University of Münster; spokesperson for the Anti-Atomtod-Ausschuss (Committee against Atomic Death).

1958
Ulrike joins the Socialist Students' Federation of Germany (SDS), participates in demonstrations against nuclear arms, and writes articles for several theoretical journals, including *Das Argument*.

January 3–4, 1959
Primarily as a result of Ulrike's interventions, the SDS manages to assert itself against the speakers of the Social Democratic Party of Germany (SPD) at the Congress against Nuclear Arms in West Berlin.

October 1959
Ulrike interrupts her studies and becomes editor of the International and Visual Arts sections of the political magazine *konkret*.

October 1959–June 1964
Ulrike is a member of the clandestine KPD.

November 15, 1959
The SPD adopts its Bad Godesberg Program, declaring itself a mass party rather than a workers' party, officially abandoning its Marxist roots and embracing the market economy. Subsequently, more than fifty thousand members are expelled from the party.

May 1961–July 1964
Ulrike is editor in chief of *konkret* and responsible for the "German Politics" section.

November 6, 1961
The SDS is expelled from the SPD because of its campaigns against Nazi judges remaining on the bench and against nuclear weapons.

December 27, 1961
Ulrike marries Klaus Rainer Röhl, the publisher of *konkret*.

September 21, 1962
Birth of Ulrike's twin daughters, Bettina and Regine.

August 1964
Ulrike steps down from the editorial staff of *konkret* but continues to work for the magazine, as well as for other periodicals, radio, and television as a freelance journalist.

January 1968
After leaving Röhl, Ulrike moves with her daughters from Hamburg to West Berlin, where she participates in the organization of the International Congress on Vietnam, held in West Berlin on February 17–18, 1968.

1968–1969

With the production of several documentaries for radio and television Ulrike takes part in campaigns against working conditions in factories and against the conditions in youth asylums. She is the coauthor of a book on women's liberation. She also produces *Bambule* (Mutiny), a made-for-TV feature film about the situation in youth asylums.

April 1969

Ulrike ends her collaboration with *konkret*.

1969–1970

Ulrike works with Petra Schelm and others in a neighborhood committee in the Märkisches Viertel, a suburban housing complex. She also lectures on "possibilities of agitation and information" at the Free University of Berlin.

May 14, 1970

Ulrike participates in the Andreas Baader prison breakout, the founding act of West Germany's first urban guerrilla group.

May 1, 1971

Publication of *The Urban Guerrilla Concept*. For the first time, the group calls itself the Red Army Faction (RAF).

July 15, 1971

Petra Schelm is killed in a shoot-out with police. Petra was one of the first members of the RAF and is the first to be killed.

March 2–3, 1972

When two RAF safehouses are discovered, Thomas Weisbecker is shot dead by a plainclothes policeman. Carmen Roll is arrested and fingerprinted under forced ether anesthesia. Manfred Grashof is arrested following a shootout in which he is seriously wounded.

March–April 1972

After an initial rumor campaign launched in July 1971, the German press resumes a campaign of insinuations, insisting that Ulrike has committed suicide or has been "liquidated" by her comrades.

May 11–24, 1972
The RAF carries out a series of bombings, including against US Army bases in Frankfurt and Heidelberg.

June 1, 1972
Jan Raspe, Holger Meins, and Andreas Baader are arrested following a shootout during which Andreas is wounded.

June 15, 1972
Ulrike is arrested.

June–July 1972
Several RAF members are arrested and placed in isolation in different prisons.

June 16, 1972–February 9, 1973
Ulrike is held in the silent wing at Cologne-Ossendorf prison.

January 17–February 16, 1973
The political prisoners' first collective hunger strike against isolation. In solidarity, on February 9–12, the lawyers stage a hunger strike in front of the Supreme Court. Ulrike is released from the silent wing, but the severe solitary confinement continues.

May 8–June 29, 1973
Second collective hunger strike against isolation. Several support committees are formed.

July 13, 1973
West Germany's attorney general orders a scintigraphy of Ulrike's brain and instructs that she be anesthetized should she not comply. The order is withdrawn on August 28 after widespread mobilizations in Germany and abroad.

December 21, 1973
For the second time, Ulrike is held in the silent wing in Cologne-Ossendorf prison. She will be there until January 3, 1974, and then once thereafter, this time with Gudrun Ensslin, from February 5 to April 28, 1974.

April 28, 1974
Ulrike and Gudrun are transferred to Stammheim prison in Stuttgart.

September 13, 1974
During the trial for the Andreas Baader prison breakout, Ulrike announces the political prisoners' third collective hunger strike.

November 9, 1974
Holger Meins dies after fifty-eight days on hunger strike.

November 11, 1974
Andreas Baader and Jan Raspe are transferred to Stammheim prison.

November 29, 1974
Ulrike is sentenced to eight years in prison for her part in the Andreas Baader prison breakout.

February 5, 1975
End of the third hunger strike.

April 24, 1975
The RAF's Holger Meins Commando occupies the West German embassy in Stockholm, demanding the release of twenty-six political prisoners. The attempt fails and results in four arrests and the deaths of two commando members, Ulrich Wessel and Siegfried Hausner.

May 21, 1975
The trial of Ulrike Meinhof, Andreas Baader, Gudrun Ensslin, and Jan Raspe begins in Stuttgart-Stammheim prison.

January 13–20, 1976
At their trial, Ulrike, Andreas, Gudrun, and Jan deliver a comprehensive statement about their politics and the development of the armed struggle.

May 4, 1976
Ulrike, Andreas, Gudrun, and Jan intervene at the trial during the debates on the defense motions regarding Germany's political role, US imperialism, and the Vietnam War.

May 9, 1976

Ulrike is found dead in her cell in Stammheim prison.

May 16, 1976

A procession of ten thousand people attends Ulrike's funeral in West Berlin.

July–August 1976

Fourteen prisoners from the RAF testify at the Stammheim trial about the structure of the group.

April 7, 1977

Attorney General Siegfried Buback, held responsible for the deaths of Holger Meins, Siegfried Hausner, and Ulrike Meinhof, is killed by the RAF's Ulrike Meinhof Commando.

Further Reading

J. Smith and André Moncourt, *The Red Army Faction: A Documentary History, Volume 1: Projectiles for the People*, Kersplebedeb and PM Press, Montreal and Oakland, 2009.

Ingrid Schubert, *Letters from Prison 1970–1977*, Kersplebedeb and PM Press, Montreal and Oakland, 2025

English translations of the RAF's texts can also be found at germanguerilla.com.

All originals of the Red Army Faction's texts can be found at the International Institute of Social History (IISH) in Amsterdam and are available at the website socialhistoryportal.org/raf, where they can be downloaded as PDFs. Included are also a large selection of texts by the prisoners and a collection of documents from internal discussions and discussions with other activists on the struggle in prison and other struggles considered relevant in this context, many of which are in English.

As to Ulrike's articles in *konkret*, most of these have been published in Ulrike Meinhof, *Aufsätze und Polemiken*, 2 volumes, Wagenbach Publishers, Berlin, 1980 and 1995. A selection in English has been published by Karin Bauer (ed.) in Ulrike Meinhof, *Everybody Talks About The Weather… We Don't*, Seven Stories Press, New York, 2011.

ABOUT PM PRESS

PM Press is an independent, radical publisher of critically
necessary books for our tumultuous times. Our aim is to
deliver bold political ideas and vital stories to all walks
of life and arm the dreamers to demand the impossible.
Founded in 2007 by a small group of people with decades
of publishing, media, and organizing experience, we have
sold millions of copies of our books, most often one at a time, face to face. We're
old enough to know what we're doing and young enough to know what's at
stake. Join us to create a better world.

PM Press
PO Box 23912
Oakland, CA 94623
www.pmpress.org

PM Press in Europe
europe@pmpress.org
www.pmpress.org.uk

FRIENDS OF PM PRESS

These are indisputably momentous times—the financial system is melting down globally and the Empire is stumbling. Now more than ever there is a vital need for radical ideas.

In the many years since its founding—and on a mere shoestring—PM Press has risen to the formidable challenge of publishing and distributing knowledge and entertainment for the struggles ahead. With hundreds of releases to date, we have published an impressive and stimulating array of literature, art, music, politics, and culture. Using every available medium, we've succeeded in connecting those hungry for ideas and information to those putting them into practice.

Friends of PM allows you to directly help impact, amplify, and revitalize the discourse and actions of radical writers, filmmakers, and artists. It provides us with a stable foundation from which we can build upon our early successes and provides a much-needed subsidy for the materials that can't necessarily pay their own way. You can help make that happen—and receive every new title automatically delivered to your door once a month—by joining as a Friend of PM Press. And, we'll throw in a free T-shirt when you sign up.

Here are your options:

- **$30 a month** Get all books and pamphlets plus a 50% discount on all webstore purchases

- **$40 a month** Get all PM Press releases (including CDs and DVDs) plus a 50% discount on all webstore purchases

- **$100 a month** Superstar—Everything plus PM merchandise, free downloads, and a 50% discount on all webstore purchases

For those who can't afford $30 or more a month, we have **Sustainer Rates** at $15, $10, and $5. Sustainers get a free PM Press T-shirt and a 50% discount on all purchases from our website.

Your Visa or Mastercard will be billed once a month, until you tell us to stop. Or until our efforts succeed in bringing the revolution around. Or the financial meltdown of Capital makes plastic redundant. Whichever comes first.

KER
SPL
EBE
DEB

Since 1998 Kersplebedeb has been an important source of radical literature and agit prop materials.

The project has a non-exclusive focus on anti-patriarchal and anti-imperialist politics, framed within an anticapitalist perspective. A special priority is given to writings regarding armed struggle in the metropole, the continuing struggles of political prisoners and prisoners of war, and the political economy of imperialism.

The Kersplebedeb website presents historical and contemporary writings by revolutionary thinkers from the anarchist and communist traditions.

Kersplebedeb can be contacted at:

Kersplebedeb
CP 63560
CCCP Van Horne
Montreal, Quebec
Canada
H3W 3H8

email: info@kersplebedeb.com
web: www.kersplebedeb.com
www.leftwingbooks.net

Kersplebedeb

Ingrid Schubert: Letters from Prison 1970-1977

Ingrid Schubert.
Edited and translated by
Gerti Wilford and Jo Tunard

ISBN: 9798887441085
$24.95   256 pages

Ingrid's letters reveal the daily struggle of a political prisoner resisting repression.

Ingrid was one of the first members of the RAF, and among the first to be imprisoned. This volume contains original letters from prison to her sister, showing her efforts to maintain her integrity, political identity, and at the same time a meaningful exchange with her family.

A collection of photos and mementos complement the letters.

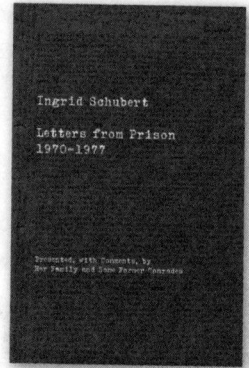

The Red Army Faction, A Documentary History - Volume 1: Projectiles For the People

Edited by J. Smith and André Moncourt
with Forewords by Russell "Maroon"
Shoats and Bill Dunne

ISBN: 978-1-60486-029-0
$34.95   736 pages

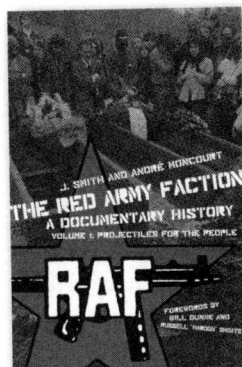

The first in a two-volume series, this is by far the most
in-depth political history of the Red Army Faction ever made available in English.

Projectiles for the People starts its story in the days following World War II,
showing how American imperialism worked hand in glove with the old pro-
Nazi ruling class, shaping West Germany into an authoritarian anticommunist
bulwark and launching pad for its aggression against Third World nations.
The volume also recounts the opposition that emerged from intellectuals,
communists, independent leftists, and then—explosively—the radical student
movement and countercultural revolt of the 1960s.

It was from this revolt that the Red Army Faction emerged, an underground
organization devoted to carrying out armed attacks within the Federal Republic
of Germany, in the view of establishing a tradition of illegal, guerilla resistance
to imperialism and state repression. Through its bombs and manifestos the RAF
confronted the state with opposition at a level many activists today might find
difficult to imagine.

For the first time ever in English, this volume presents all of the manifestos
and communiqués issued by the RAF between 1970 and 1977, from Andreas
Baader's prison break, through the 1972 May Offensive and the 1975 hostage-
taking in Stockholm, to the desperate, and tragic, events of the "German
Autumn" of 1977. The RAF's three main manifestos—*The Urban Guerilla Concept*,
Serve the People, and *Black September*—are included, as are important interviews
with *Spiegel* and *le Monde Diplomatique*, and a number of communiqués and
court statements explaining their actions.

Providing the background information that readers will require to understand
the context in which these events occurred, separate thematic sections deal
with the 1976 murder of Ulrike Meinhof in prison, the 1977 Stammheim murders,
the extensive use of psychological operations and false-flag attacks to discredit
the guerilla, the state's use of sensory deprivation torture and isolation wings,
and the prisoners' resistance to this, through which they inspired their own
supporters and others on the left to take the plunge into revolutionary action.

The Red Army Faction, A Documentary History: Volume 2: Dancing with Imperialism

Edited J. Smith and André Moncourt with an Introduction by Ward Churchill

ISBN: 978-1-60486-030-6
$26.95   480 pages

The long-awaited *Volume 2* of the first-ever English-language study of the Red Army Faction—West Germany's most notorious urban guerillas—covers the period immediately following the organization's near-total decimation in 1977. This work includes the details of the guerilla's operations, and its communiqués and texts, from 1978 up until the 1984 offensive.

This was a period of regrouping and reorientation for the RAF, with its previous focus on freeing its prisoners replaced by an anti-NATO orientation. This was in response to the emergence of a new radical youth movement in the Federal Republic, the Autonomen, and an attempt to renew its ties to the radical left. The possibilities and perils of an armed underground organization relating to the broader movement are examined, and the RAF's approach is contrasted to the more fluid and flexible practice of the Revolutionary Cells. At the same time, the history of the 2nd of June Movement (2JM), an eclectic guerilla group with its roots in West Berlin, is also evaluated, especially in light of the split that led to some 2JM members officially disbanding the organization and rallying to the RAF. Finally, the RAF's relationship to the East German Stasi is examined, as is the abortive attempt by West Germany's liberal intelligentsia to defuse the armed struggle during Gerhard Baum's tenure as Minister of the Interior.

Dancing with Imperialism will be required reading for students of the First World guerilla, those with interest in the history of European protest movements, and all who wish to understand the challenges of revolutionary struggle.

"This collection is not simply a documentary of the West German revolutionary Left at a particular point in the Cold War 1970s. It is more important for the insights it provides into the challenges, obstacles, and opportunities of waging armed struggle within the context of a wealthy, well-resourced, Western capitalist state. In this, the experiences and activities of the RAF are unique in the lessons they might teach organizers in Western capitalist milieus. In our own context, it is likely that future conditions of radical social change, and certainly revolutionary struggles, will more closely approximate those engaged by the RAF in 1970s West Germany than the much more influential examples of Russia in 1917 or Spain in 1936."
—Jeff Shantz, *Upping the Anti*